Live Lent!

Year B

By Sr. Theresa Rickard, O.P.

Weekday reflections by Deacon Charles Paolino

D0831312

Excerpts from the English translation of Lectionary for Mass © 1969, 1981, 1997, International Commission on English in the Liturgy Corporation (ICEL). All rights reserved.

RENEW International gratefully acknowledges contributors to this work: Martin Lang and Trish Sullivan Vanni.

NIHIL OBSTAT
    Reverend Christopher M. Ciccarino, S.S.L., S.T.D.

IMPRIMATUR
    Joseph W. Cardinal Tobin, C.Ss.R.
    Archbishop of Newark

Cover design by Ruth Markworth
Interior Design Consultant: Blue Willow Publishing Works
Interior Page Layout by Clara Baumann
Cover photo © Radu Razvan Gheorghe | Dreamstime.com

ISBN: 978-1-62063-136-2

RENEW International
    1232 George Street
    Plainfield, NJ 07062-1717
    www.renewintl.org

Printed and bound in the United States of America

Contents

LIVE LENT!

During a retreat, I met a young woman who was a scientist. She was a committed Catholic, and she loved her work, but she told me that after attending church on Ash Wednesday, she had been concerned about returning to the lab with that mark on her forehead. She prayed for the courage to do so, and she went back to work where a co-worker, seeing the ashes, asked her, "Do you still believe in that stuff?"

"Yes," she replied, "I do believe."

That young woman, who courageously affirmed her faith in the face of someone else's doubt, or even scorn, showed that she was prepared to not only believe but live what she believed. And in recent decades the Church has encouraged us to use the season of Lent as an occasion to refresh, or kick start, our disposition to do the same.

That is why we at RENEW chose the title of this book—to challenge the common perception that we observe Lent—that it ends after 40 days, and then we go back to life as usual, drinking those two glasses of wine each night, eating a box of chocolates a week, going back to the couch instead of to the gym, or hitting the snooze button for 15 minutes instead of making time for morning prayer.

Nor is the Lenten challenge designed to merely change a few habits. It is a call to transformation, to becoming a new person in Christ Jesus. The life cycle of the caterpillar is a good metaphor that illustrates this difference: The insect that withdraws into the chrysalis doesn't emerge as a tweaked caterpillar but as a totally new creature. We are called to open ourselves to the action of the Holy Spirit and intentionally live Lent so that after the 40 days we will be not just tweaked but transformed into who God desires us to be—our true selves, living with purpose and meaning.

Pope Francis eloquently expressed this idea: "Once again, Lent comes to make its prophetic appeal, to remind us that it is possible to create something new within ourselves and around ourselves." We create that "something new" when we live, as Jesus lived, lives of mercy, compassion, and justice, giving witness to and practicing what we proclaim.

Lent is the season to recognize the call that we all received at baptism, the call to live every day as missionary disciples of Christ so that we may come to say with St. Paul, "It is no longer I who live, but it is Christ who lives in me" (Galatians 2:20).

Preparing for Lent

For me, the Lenten season has always been a time to refocus on God and get my life in right order. I want to Live Lent! so I can live faith with greater integrity and in deeper communion with God and my neighbor. I have come to realize that Lent is not so much about giving up things as it is about seizing the opportunity to be all that God has called me to be—a holy, healthy, and loving person—a disciple of Jesus Christ committed to transforming my faith into real-life action.

So, let me suggest not ways to fast but things to do and things not to do this Lent. First, things to do:

Consciously surrender to God. Whenever we say the Lord's Prayer we ask that God's will be done on earth. And Lent reminds us that leading a Christian life means setting aside our will—our desires and wishes and priorities—and asking God to help us behave only according to his will.

Let go of old self-images. Imitating Jesus, who died on the cross, is to empty ourselves of ego and see ourselves as who we really are— creatures totally dependent on our Creator, but also living reflections of God's love and compassion. We are flawed and fabulous, and we need to let go of denigrating ourselves and old tapes that tell us that we are not good enough or smart enough or attractive enough. Lent is a time to see ourselves clearly—as Father Richard Rohr's says, to find our true selves, our God selves, our Christ selves.

Don't starve yourself. Lent Focus on engendering life from within. No matter what we own or what we lack in the way of material possessions or wealth, our greatest gifts to each other, to the world at large, will always come from within us. Be conscious of the Holy Spirit encouraging your powers of love, compassion, and justice; realize the potential in these gifts; find ways to use these gifts to bless the lives of others in large ways and small.

Ask for the grace of transformation. Pray each day that you will emerge from this Lenten experience as a new person. Leave the details of your renewal up to God, and thank him for his grace.

And now, things not to do:

Don't give up. Instead of giving up something for Lent, try doing something that will bring you closer to God. Perhaps attend Mass during the week, spend time reflecting on the daily or Sunday readings by yourself and with others by using this book, experience the beauty of God's creation by taking walks, make donations to your favorite charities, volunteer at the local food bank, light candles and say prayers for the people you know who are struggling. If you still decide to give something up, do it for someone else. For example, if you give up wine for Lent, each time you decline to take wine, pray for someone who struggles with an addiction to alcohol.

Don't sweat it. Whatever it is you commit to do this Lent, the point isn't to do it perfectly. Give it your best, but if you slip up, accept that as a reminder that you are not perfect. Only God is perfect. Say a prayer, and start again.

Don't starve yourself. Lent isn't about going on a diet or losing weight—it's about the conversion of hearts. Eat healthy, get some exercise, but don't succumb to our culture's obsession with physical appearances. Again, if you want to give up sweets, do it for someone who is seriously overweight.

Don't make it more difficult than it is. The three pillars of Lent are prayer, fasting, and almsgiving. Find simple ways to pray, fast, and give to those who are poor.

Don't hold back. Lent will present you with many opportunities to convert your heart and your life, to heal broken relationships, and to grow closer to God. When you find yourself presented with such an opportunity, embrace it.

So this Lent don't give up, don't sweat it, don't starve yourself, don't make it more difficult than it is, and, most especially, don't hold back! Live Lent! so you can live a more authentic faith long after these 40 days have passed.

40 Days to Live Lent!

A good Lent begins with a plan. Just as we carefully plan for big events in our personal lives, such as a graduation or a wedding, Lent invites us to make our hearts ready for remembering Jesus' passion and celebrating Jesus' resurrection. The best way to celebrate Jesus resurrection is to live more fully Christ's life in the here and now.

What are some actions this Lent that can deepen your relationship with God, make you more aware of God's presence in your life, and help you to be kinder, more loving, to others? Reflect on your life and where you are in your relationship with God. Which relationship in your life most needs forgiveness and God's healing presence? What are you doing for people who are poor and needy? What bad habit is keeping you away from God? What do you need to change?

Pray about it; ask God. We can't make changes in our lives without God's grace. Willpower is never enough. Now, write down simple actions under each of the three areas we are invited to act on during Lent: prayer, fasting, and almsgiving (giving to those in need and supporting our parish and other worthy organizations). Many parishes participate in Catholic Relief Services Rice Bowl program through which millions of Catholics in the United States apply the Lenten pillars of praying, fasting, and almsgiving to help alleviate hunger around the world. See if your parish does this, or help to establish the program in your parish. For more information, go to www.crsricebowl.org.

Remember, we are called to live Lent so we can live faith not only during these 40 days but every day henceforth.

Jot down the commitments you will make in each of these areas. Remember, keep it simple and doable. Review your Lenten commitments each Sunday during Lent, and make adjustments. Don't give up; keep at it.

Prayer:

_____

_____

_____

_____

_____

_____

_____

Fasting:

_____

_____

_____

_____

_____

_____

_____

Almsgiving:

_____

_____

_____

_____

_____

_____

_____

Ash Wednesday

 Pray

"Give me back the joy of your salvation, and a willing spirit sustain in me." (Psalm 51:12)

 Read *Matthew 6: 1-6, 16-18*

Summary: *"(W)hen you fast, anoint your head and wash your face, so that you may not appear to be fasting, except to your Father who is hidden. And your Father who sees what is hidden will repay you."*
(Matthew 6:17-18)

Spend two minutes in silence. Then repeat this passage from Scripture, and let it speak to your heart.

 Meditation

I grew up under "the old system." In the 1940s and '50s the Lenten fast still ended at noon on Holy Saturday. For me, it was the lifting of a great burden, because my family had a grocery store where I had easy access to candy, ice cream, and soda. But when Ash Wednesday arrived, I was cut off. So on Holy Saturday, I was sure to be in the store by 11:45, watching the clock while both hands crept toward 12.

I scrupulously observed the fast, although I could have snitched a candy bar or a Popsicle when the store was closed and my parents were distracted. There was no heroism in this; I observed the fast—and went to confession on Saturday and Mass on Sunday—because I was afraid not to. When the fast was over, I felt the way an athlete must feel when he has completed a triathlon.

In the decades since then I have learned that fasting is not an ordeal to test our resolve or punishment for our sins or self-denial that prepares us to better enjoy self-indulgence. I have learned that rather than delivering us safe and sound to our routine, Lent should unsettle us in a way that lasts long after the clock strikes twelve.

As Pope Francis has explained, fasting makes sense only if it fine tunes our awareness of the material and spiritual poverty in which so many live and heightens our motivation to use wisely and share the resources God has given us.

The holy mark we receive today will fade, but we can resolve as we receive it not to be content so long as a brother or sister is cold or hungry.

Live Lent!

I will make an account of my resources—time, talent, skills, funds, and material goods—and honestly consider what part of these I could reasonably share with someone in need.

 Pray

Generous God, we thank you for all that you have given us. May the fast and prayer of this holy season help us value your gifts— not only as blessings in our own lives but as resources that we can share with those who are in need who are our sisters and brothers. We ask this through Jesus Christ, our Lord. Amen.

Thursday after Ash Wednesday

 Pray

"I have set before you life and death, the blessing and the curse. … Choose life, then, that you and your descendants may live, …"
(Deuteronomy 30:19)

 Read *Luke 9:22-25*

Summary: *"For whoever wishes to save his life will lose it, but whoever loses his life for my sake will save it."*
(Luke 9:24)

Spend two minutes in silence. Then repeat this passage from Scripture, and let it speak to your heart.

 Meditation

One of my college books included a passage written by the British author W. Somerset Maugham. "To myself," Maugham wrote, "I am the most important person in the world … but from the standpoint of common sense, I am of no consequence whatever. It would have made small difference to the universe if I had never existed." That passage made me realize that, at times, I too, saw the world as revolving around me—an illusion shared by hundreds of millions of human beings.

Deny your very self, Jesus says, and doing that may begin with recognizing that no one person is the center of all that is. But that shouldn't lead anyone to the conclusion that he or she is "of no consequence whatever." On the contrary, the self-denial that Jesus calls us to is the first step toward committing all of our gifts, not to our own comfort or influence or social standing, but to the wellbeing of our closest neighbors and of the world at large.

Whatever its problems, the world is a far better place because of the unselfish actions of countless people who lost their lives, as Jesus meant it, rather than saving them—who gave away parts of their lives in order to bless the lives of others. The fact that most of those selfless people are anonymous and perhaps soon forgotten does not reduce the importance to life on earth of each of them individually and all of them together.

As Pope Francis has written: "No single act of love for God will be lost, no generous effort is meaningless. …"

Live Lent!

I will spend time today recalling the gifts and favors large and small with which others have blessed me and made my life better. I will pray in gratitude for the gift givers and their gifts, and I will pray for the will to bless others in the same way.

Pray

*Lord, Jesus Christ, help me to imitate your life, not focusing
on myself but freely devoting my energies and resources to
building up the lives of others. Amen.*

Friday after Ash Wednesday

 Pray

*"My sacrifice, O God, is a contrite spirit; a heart contrite and
humbled, O God, you will not spurn." (Psalm 51:17)*

 Read *Matthew 9:14-15*

Summary: *"Then the disciples of John approached Jesus and said,
'Why do we and the Pharisees fast [much],
but your disciples do not fast?'"*
Matthew 9:14

*Spend two minutes in silence. Then repeat this passage from Scripture, and
let it speak to your heart.*

 Meditation

When the playwright-director George Abbot was 106 years old, he
attended the opening of a Broadway revival of Damn Yankees, for
which he had written the book forty years before. As Abbott walked
down the aisle, the audience stood and applauded, and Abbott said to
his companion, "There must be someone important here." There was,
indeed. The audience knew it, and the audience celebrated.

Unlike that astute audience, the folks we read about in today's
gospel passage missed out on an even bigger reason to celebrate: the
presence of Jesus among them. Not only did they fail to recognize him
as the long-awaited Messiah, but they failed to accept even the truth of
his message of unconditional compassion and love.

Referring to himself as the bridegroom, Jesus said that those who walked with him and learned from him had reason to rejoice. But he was also preparing them for the time when he would no longer be physically present among them, and they would be left to live as he had taught them and spread his Gospel. Then they would fast, and now we fast—through prayer, penance, self-denial, and charity. Through our fasting we put aside both the distractions of a wasteful and noisy world and the preoccupation with our own comfort and convenience. Through our fasting we remember how much he sacrificed to overcome the consequences of sin and death and to offer the hope of eternal life. Through our fasting we see more clearly our mission as his disciples: to be his presence in the lives of so many who need sustenance, solace, and healing.

Live Lent!

I will pray about how I am capable of making Jesus present in the lives of others, especially those whom I find unappealing or with whom I have differences.

 Pray

Lord Jesus, help me to clearly see during Lent and throughout the year how I may make you present to the least of my brothers and sisters, treating them as you would treat them, so that they, too, can celebrate your promise of salvation and eternal life. Amen.

Saturday after Ash Wednesday

 Pray

"For you, O Lord, are good and forgiving, abounding in kindness to all who call upon you." (Psalm 86:15)

Read *Luke 5:27-32*

Summary: *"Those who are healthy do not need a physician, but*

---

the sick do. I have not come to call the righteous to repentance but sinners." *(Luke 5:31b-32)*

Spend two minutes in silence. Then repeat this passage from Scripture, and let it speak to your heart.

 Meditation

One of the personalities in the cast of characters of my childhood had the quaint name Dr. Owsley Duncan. Dr. Duncan was, in effect, the primary-care physician for my grandparents; when I was a boy, he seemed to me to be ancient. He lived in a Victorian house in a city adjacent to my hometown and kept his money in a chamois bag in the bottom drawer of an oak roll-top desk.

Like many doctors five and six decades ago, Dr. Duncan made house calls. He didn't drive, so he took a bus from his street to ours—a distance of about four miles. He did what Jesus said a physician did: he went where he was needed.

In that sense, Dr. Duncan himself was a metaphor for Jesus, who went out of his way to encounter people who needed healing, the folks often summed up by the Pharisees as "tax collectors and sinners." That was the great gift that Jesus gave to the people of his time and still gives to us—that when our spirits are ailing or in pain, he does not wait passively for us to seek him out but makes himself available to us in the sacraments, in the Gospels, and in the intimacy of prayer.

For that reason, we can undertake our Lenten practices with confidence that Jesus Christ will not be watching from a distance but will be present as we pray, as we fast, and as we perform acts of charity and justice, and will touch us with the grace that only he can give.

Live Lent!

I will spend some quiet time each day this week considering one way in which I would like to live more in tune with the Gospel and opening my heart and mind to the healing touch of Jesus.

Pray

Lord Jesus, you went out to bless those who acknowledged their failings, and you invited them to follow you. Help me to see the ways in which I need your help in order to be a more faithful disciple. Amen.

First Sunday of Lent

"The kingdom of God is at hand."

Suggested Environment

A small table with a burning candle and a Bible opened to the gospel reading for this session. Consider decorating the table with violet, the liturgical color of the Lenten season. Place a bowl containing sand on the table to suggest the desert.

Liturgical Readings for the
First Sunday of Lent

GENESIS 9:8-15
"I will establish my covenant with you."

PSALM 25:4-5,6-7,8-9
"Good and upright is the Lord."

1 PETER 3:18-22
"Christ suffered for sins … that he might lead you to God."

MARK 1:12-15
"This is the time of fulfillment."

Focus

God never gives up on us when we turn away.

Opening Song (To download, visit ocp.org/renew-music.)

"Loving and Forgiving," Scott Soper

Opening Prayer

Divide the group in two, and pray together from Psalm 25, with everyone repeating the response:

R. **Your ways, O Lord, are love and truth to those who keep your covenant.**

Side 1: Your ways, O Lord, make known to me;
teach me your paths,
guide me in your truth and teach me,
for you are God my Savior.

R. **Your ways, O Lord, are love and truth to those who keep your covenant.**

Side 2: Remember that your compassion, O Lord,
and your love are from of old.
In your kindness remember me,
because of your goodness, O Lord.

R. **Your ways, O Lord, are love and truth to those who keep your covenant.**

Side 1: Good and upright is the Lord,
thus he shows sinners the way.
He guides the humble to justice,
and he teaches the humble his way.

R. **Your ways, O Lord, are love and truth to those who keep your covenant.**

All: **Amen.**

The Gospel of the Lord

"Repent, and believe in the Gospel."

Read aloud Mark 1:12-15

Reflect

What word, phrase, or image from the scripture reading touches your heart or connects to your experience? Share with the group, and/or write your response here:

_____

_____

_____

_____

Old Testament Connections

Mark's community, steeped in biblical narratives, hear that Jesus spent forty days in the wilderness, and they recall that the Israelites wandered and were tested in the desert for forty years (Num 10:11-21:34), Moses fasted for forty days and nights as he wrote the Ten Commandments (Ex. 34:8), and Elijah fasted for the same time as he walked to Mt. Horeb (1 Kings 19:8). The number "forty" is highly symbolic in all biblical literature, representing "a long time," especially a time of trial or testing.

For Jewish people, the wilderness of the desert was a place where their confidence in God was shaken and tested. The desert was not a success story for them. They succumbed to temptation and turned their back on God—the God who had entered a covenant with them after the Flood. ... (Genesis 9:8-15). God guided the Jews through the wilderness and fed them on their difficult journey with both physical and spiritual food. Even when they turned away from God, God remained faithful to his covenant love, eventually leading them out of the wilderness and into the Promised Land (Joshua 1-24). By the time their desert wanderings were over, the people of Israel had come to know that even with their infidelities, the God who initiated a relationship with them would always be faithful and would not give up on them.

Reflect

Why is the Exodus event (the journey from oppression in Egypt through the desert to the Promised land) such a key story for the Jewish people?

What is the good news for you in the way God responded to the failings of the Hebrew people during their difficult journey through the wilderness? Share with the group, or write your response here:

_____

_____

_____

_____

Meditation

There is a classic tale about two monks traveling to visit a monastery in a nearby town. While passing through the town they observe a young woman attempting to step out of her carriage, but she is frustrated, because the recent rain has created deep puddles. She is angry and impatient at her attendants, because they stand there with her bags but do not act quickly to assist her.

The younger monk notices the angry and impatient woman and moves on. The older monk quickly picks her up and carries her across the water to dry land. She doesn't thank the monk; she brushes him aside and goes on her way.

As they continue their journey, the young monk is brooding. After several hours, unable to hold his silence, he speaks out: "That woman was very arrogant and rude, but you carried her to dry land anyway! Then she didn't even thank you!" "I set the woman down hours ago," the older monk replies. "Why are you still carrying her?"

The older monk was free. He did the right thing and was unattached to the outcome. He did not need affirmation or gratitude from that woman or from anyone else. The older monk at that moment was his "true self," and the divine shone through him.

I am sure the wise old monk was tempted to walk away from the ungrateful woman and to be angry when she didn't show gratitude. However, he chose instead to do a kind act—he set the woman down and moved on. This is one of the temptations many of us struggle with—the need to be affirmed. How many times have I said or heard others complain, "and that person didn't even thank me."

Fr. Thomas Keating, a Trappist monk, describes the false self as three energy centers within us that motivate us to act to satisfy our ego's exaggerated needs. These energy centers emerge in early childhood, when we are most vulnerable, as our attempt to cope whenever we experience a sense of depravation or fear. The three primary energy centers of the false self are an exaggerated need for security, esteem, and power or control. Most of our personal issues are related to our attempts to satisfy these exaggerated needs by trying to accumulate whatever symbols of security, esteem, and power make us feel good.

Fr. Keating is putting into contemporary terms the same thing that the gospel writers addressed two thousand years ago, through this story of the temptation of Jesus.

In Mark's brief account of the temptation, he simply says Jesus was driven into the desert by the Spirit and was tempted. We discover the details of the temptations in the longer versions found in the Gospels of Matthew and Luke. First, the tempter offers Jesus food to satisfy his hunger. He next offers Jesus a dramatic act guaranteed to raise esteem for him—to give him "rock star" status as he begins his public ministry. From the pinnacle of the temple, the most visible sight in Jerusalem, Jesus can safely throw himself to the ground. Finally, the tempter offers Jesus the title of king and power over all the kingdoms of the earth. Jesus turns away from each of these false offers. Instead, Jesus embraces God the Father as his source of perfect security, perfect love, and perfect power.

Accepting security, esteem, and power as gifts rather than trying to achieve them on our own is a fundamental exercise of faith. We, like the people of Israel, like Jesus, have had the experience of being thrown into the wilderness. We might call these times crisis periods that test our faith and challenge us to separate from an old way of being and enter a time of transformation. Jesus emerged from the desert victorious. His victory is not for him alone but for each of us who trusts in God's unconditional love. Amid life's struggles, God promises to walk with us through the chaos of the moment and carry us to safety; only the graciousness of God can deliver us. And even if we turn away from God, he will not give up on us. Like the older monk, he will carry us—again and again.

Reflect

How do you identify with the younger monk? The older monk?

_____

_____

_____

_____

Which of the three energies of the false self (security, affirmation, power/control) do you most struggle with?

_____

_____

_____

_____

What time of conflict, struggle, or chaos challenged you to grow in your faith? How did God accompany you? Did he send "human angels" to support you?

_____

_____

_____

_____

Who is in most need of your support right now?

_____

_____

_____

_____

Live Lent!

† Reach out to a person in most need of your support

† Do an act of kindness for a person who in the past has not shown gratitude; expect no return.

† Thirst is a critical problem that affects scores of millions of people in the world who lack access to potable water. Catholic Relief Services supports initiatives that help bring clean and proper sanitation to areas in need. Consider donating to this program. You can find out at crs.org/wash what the program does and how you can contribute.

† Spend time prayerfully reviewing your Lenten Plan, making any adjustments that you think are needed.

Closing Prayer

Pray together:

Gracious God, accompany me as I navigate the conflicts and struggles in my life. Help me to trust in your covenant love and your desire to lift me up when I stumble in the face of temptation. Thank you for your faithful love and for never giving up on me. Guide me through this Lenten season to a renewed and deeper relationship with you. Amen.

Looking Ahead

To prepare for the Second Sunday of Lent, read:

• Mark 9:2-10

• Session Two: Transformed by Christ

Monday

 Pray

"You shall love your neighbor as yourself. I am the LORD." (Leviticus 19:18b)

 Read *Matthew 25:31–46*

Summary: *"Amen I say to you, what you did not do for one of these least ones, you did not do for me."*
(Matthew 25:40b)

Spend two minutes in silence. Then repeat this passage from Scripture, and let it speak to your heart.

 Meditation

When my mother was in her seventies, she surprised us by enrolling as a "foster grandmother" at a center for mentally challenged people. Foster grandmothers helped the staff care for the youngest residents, and Mom worked with the babies in the nursery.

Mom had been a homemaker for most of her adult life and then worked in the office of a company that serviced book publishers; she had never come in direct contact with mentally challenged people. And yet, this new experience gave her some of the greatest joy of her life. She loved to tell us about the children (who sometimes kicked her and vomited on her); she showed us pictures of them, cheerfully described their antics, and called them her "little angels." Mom, a woman of faith, didn't seem to think she was doing these children a favor; she simply extended to them the same generosity she had been extending to family, friends, and strangers throughout her life. On the day of judgment described by Jesus in the Gospel of Matthew, Mom might be among those who ask the Son of Man, "When did we see you in need and care for you?"

The Gospel implies that we all are called to cultivate in ourselves that same frame of mind, caring for those in need, not out of a sense of obligation, not out of a desire for praise or reward, but out of a conviction that all human beings, no matter how distinguished by want or illness or disability, share the humanity of Jesus himself. To love them is to love him.

Live Lent!

I will consider this question: Who are the "least" of Jesus' brothers and sisters in my parish or community and what is my relationship with them?

 Pray

Lord Jesus, through your incarnation you became the brother of us all, the living embodiment of the love God has for his people. Help me to be a reflection of that love by embracing all people, without distinction, as my brothers and sisters. Amen.

Tuesday

 Pray

"The Lord has eyes for the just, and ears for their cry." (Psalm 34:16)

 Read *Matthew 6:7-15*

Summary: *"If you forgive men their transgressions, your heavenly Father will forgive you. But if you do not forgive men, neither will your Father forgive your transgressions."* (Matthew 6:14-15)

Spend two minutes in silence. Then repeat this passage from Scripture, and let it speak to your heart.

 **Meditation**

In both my parish ministry and in my profession, I have spent a lot of time talking with adults about the Gospels. Something I hear repeatedly is that adults find that forgiveness is one of the most challenging aspects of our Christian faith. Many folks find it hard to accept the idea that God will unconditionally forgive their sins, and even more find it hard to unconditionally extend their own forgiveness. This last applies both to those who have offended or hurt them personally and to those who have offended their sense of justice—such as brutal dictators, terrorists, or other violent criminals.

Accepting what Jesus meant when he taught us to "forgive those who trespass against us" begins with accepting the fact that God is not only willing but eager to forgive us when we turn back to him, that God doesn't hold out forgiveness as a kind of bait to prompt us to behave in a certain way but rather as a gift that he wants to give us. That is how Jesus expects us to forgive even those who may seem to us to be beyond the reach of God's grace and, therefore, our compassion. It is a radical idea—forgiving even the worst offenders—but it is what Jesus taught and what Jesus himself did even as he was dying on the cross.

During the quiet times of Lent, may we recall that just as Jesus shared with us our human nature we share with him an unlimited capacity to forgive.

Live Lent!

I will reflect on whom I find most difficult to forgive, and I will commit myself in prayer to let go of my anger and commend such people to God's judgment and mercy.

 Pray

Lord Jesus, as you suffered on the cross you asked your Father to forgive those who were unjustly putting you to death. Following your example, I ask forgiveness for all who have offended or harmed me in any way, and forgiveness for the times when I have harbored resentment or anger toward others. May God have mercy on us all. Amen.

Wednesday

 Pray

"For you are not pleased with sacrifices; should I offer a burnt offering, you would not accept it. My sacrifice, O God, is a contrite spirit; a heart contrite and humbled, O God, you will not spurn." (Psalm 51:18-19)

 Read *Luke 11:29-32*

Summary: "While still more people gathered in the crowd, Jesus said to them, 'This generation is an evil generation; it seeks a sign, but no sign will be given it, except the sign of Jonah. Just as Jonah became a sign to the Ninevites, so will the Son of Man be to this generation.'" *(Luke 11:29-30)*

Spend two minutes in silence. Then repeat this passage from Scripture, and let it speak to your heart.

 **Meditation**

I met Monsignor William N. Wall in the late 1950s when I was an altar server at my parish church in New Jersey. He got my attention because he wore khaki pants and sneakers under his cassock, the first priest I knew who wore anything but black clerical clothing. He was not to be trifled with; he frequently paused during Mass and glared at people who were disruptive and sometimes even bluntly rebuked them.

More importantly, in a nearby city he founded and ran the Mount Carmel Guild where he helped indigent men who were addicted to alcohol. He took these men in, cleaned them up, and put them to work. In my young life Monsignor Wall provided the first example of ministry going outside the walls of the church and the boundaries of the parish and touching people regardless of their backgrounds.

Monsignor Wall was a no-nonsense guy. He didn't wait for signs to convince him of Jesus' authority; he simply took the Gospel to heart and got busy living it in the real world. He was an extraordinary man, and yet he was doing in his way what Jesus calls us all to do in our ways. Jesus said the only sign for the people of his generation would be the "sign of Jonah." That sign was the resurrection. As we anticipate our celebration of Jesus' triumph over sin and death, we need no other sign to impel us to go into the world as his missionary disciples.

Live Lent!

I will reflect on who or what has been a sign for me as to how I should live as a disciple of Christ. What has that sign inspired me to do?

 Pray

Lord Jesus, your sacrifice and resurrection are signs to me that life and good can triumph over death and sin. Help me to follow your example and that of your disciples through the ages so that I, too, may be an instrument through which you heal and comfort the world. Amen.

Thursday

 Pray

"I will worship at your holy temple and give thanks to your name, Because of your kindness and your truth . . . ." (Psalm 138:2)

 Read *Matthew 7:7-12*

Summary: *"Would one of you hand your son a stone when he asks for a loaf…?"* (Matthew 7:9)

Spend two minutes in silence. Then repeat this passage from Scripture, and let it speak to your heart.

Meditation

As the credits roll in the 1966 film *Alfie*, Cher sings the theme written by

Hal David and Burt Bacharach.

Alfie is about a limousine driver who learns the hard way the consequences of his cavalier attitude toward women.

David's lyrics ask whether we are "meant to get more than we give" or, rather, are we "meant to be kind?" The next line says: "And if life belongs only to the strong, Alfie, what will you lend on an old golden rule?"

The reference is to the statement Jesus makes at the end of today's gospel reading: "Treat others as you would have them treat you: this sums up the law and the prophets."

This maxim has been known as "the golden rule" since at least 1604.

Jesus himself undoubtedly read this instruction in the Book of Leviticus, written hundreds of years before his birth. The same idea has been expounded for centuries. For example, the Greek philosopher Pittacus, more than five hundred years before Jesus was born, taught, "Do not do to your neighbor that which you would not suffer from him" and the Chinese sage Confucius, who died in 479 B.C., counseled, "What you do not want others to do to you do not do to others." And the Jewish sage Hillel (d. 10 AD) famously taught, "What is hateful to you, do not do to your neighbor. That is the whole Torah; the rest is the explanation of this—Go and study it!" (*Shabbat*, 31a).

This idea is a matter of common sense—so much so that it almost seems unnecessary to say it. And yet most of the mischief in the world, from personal slights to terror attacks to open warfare, is possible only to the degree that human beings ignore this rule.

If we were to do only one thing as an observance of Lent, we could not do better than to reflect on how well—in our relationships at home, among our neighbors, in our workplaces—we keep this simple but "golden" rule.

Live Lent!

While I'm driving, while I'm dealing with store clerks, while I'm giving or taking instructions at work or school, while I'm interacting with my parents or children, I will intentionally ask myself, "Is this how I would want to be treated?"

 Pray

Lord Jesus, you were our model when you treated people with compassion, patience, and mercy. Help us to keep your example in mind as we touch the lives of other people each day. Amen.

Friday

 Pray

"If you, O Lord, mark iniquities, Lord, who can stand? But with you is forgiveness, that you may be revered." (Psalm 130:3-4)

 Read *Matthew 5:20-26*

Summary: *"You have heard that it was said to your ancestors, You shall not kill; and whoever kills will be liable to judgment. But I say to you, whoever is angry with his brother will be liable to judgment. ..."*
(Matthew 5:21-22a)

Spend two minutes in silence. Then repeat this passage from Scripture, and let it speak to your heart.

 Meditation

Most of us have no problem applying to our lives the literal meaning of the Fifth Commandment, "You shall not kill." But Jesus raised the bar considerably by saying that we must not even harbor anger against each other. Letting go of slights, betrayals, unfaithfulness, and violence is, indeed, challenging. But it is what we are called to, as we learn from Jesus in more than one passage of the Gospels.

I sometimes use the example of Corrie ten Boom, a Christian

woman who lived in the Netherlands during the Holocaust and who joined her father and other relatives to hide Jewish people from the Nazis. Eventually the whole ten Boom family was arrested, and Corrie and her sister Betsie were sent to a concentration camp at Ravensbrück, Germany, where Betsie died. In 1947, Corrie spoke in Munich on the theme of forgiveness. After her talk, a man from the audience approached her, and she recognized him as a guard at the concentration camp. He thanked her for her talk and remarked that it was good to know that God forgives our sins. He acknowledged that he had been a guard at Ravensbrück and explained that he had become a Christian. He offered his hand to Carrie who, as she later wrote, was filled with revulsion. But her own message to that audience welled up in her, and she grasped the man's hand and told him she forgave him.

Most of us will never have to forgive an offense of that magnitude, and yet forgiveness even on that level is what Jesus calls us to.

Live Lent!

I will spend time in prayer about any anger or resentment I may be entertaining against another person. Remembering that Jesus forgave even those who put him to death, I will try to replace my rancor with a gesture of conciliation—a note, a card, or a phone call.

 Pray

Dear Jesus, you gave us the most sublime example of forgiveness by praying for those who were taking your life. Help me to imitate you by forgiving those who have wounded me, no matter how serious the offense. May I always be a source of the peace that you desire for the world. Amen.

Saturday

 Pray

"You have commanded that your precepts be diligently kept. Oh,

that I might be firm in the ways of keeping your statutes!" (Psalm 119:4-5)

 Read Matthew 5:43-48

Summary: "But I say to you, love your enemies, and pray for those who persecute you, that you may be children of your heavenly Father, for he makes his sun rise on the bad and the good, and causes rain to fall on the just and the unjust." (Matthew 5:44-45)

Spend two minutes in silence. Then repeat this passage from Scripture, and let it speak to your heart.

Meditation

When Durham, North Carolina faced school integration in the 1970s, Ann Atwater was a leader in the black community and C.P. Ellis was head of the local Ku Klux Klan. Feelings between them were so bitter that Ann once took out a knife to attack C.P. during a public gathering but was stopped by her friends.

When a court ordered Durham's schools to integrate, the two agreed to co-chair community meetings to decide how to implement the order. Forced into each other's company, Ann and C.P., both poor, discovered their common interests, including their concern for the safety and education of their children and their impotence in a local society dominated by white and black middle classes.

Because of their dialogue, C.P. realized that the black people he had despised were really fellow travelers on life's journey. He publicly destroyed his KKK card and became a leader of black and white unions in Durham. Ann and he became faithful friends.

It is simple to respond to this story by calling it extraordinary. But as Christians, we are called to do the extraordinary, if that means recognizing the humanity we share with everyone on earth, even enemies of our nation and our way of life. We cannot come face to face with all of them or personally influence them the way Ann Atwater influenced C.P. Ellis; however, we can love them as brothers and sisters created in God's image and pray that God will inspire them to find fulfillment in ways that honor his law and human dignity.

Live Lent!

I will ask the Holy Spirit to help me think of all people, including those I regard as enemies, first of all as brothers and sisters responding to the circumstances of their lives. I will consciously include in my prayers people and groups whose philosophies or behaviors I abhor, asking God to inspire them to more humane and fruitful lives.

 Pray

Lord Jesus, you taught us with the story of the Good Samaritan that our "enemy" is also our neighbor. Help me to take that lesson to heart and to pray only that all people might eventually act on the best impulses of the human nature our Creator gave us. Amen.

Second Sunday of Lent

Transformed by Christ

Suggested Environment

A small table with a burning candle—or perhaps several candles as an image of the radiance of Christ's divinity—and a Bible opened to the gospel reading for this session. Consider decorating the table with violet, the liturgical color of the Lenten season

Liturgical Readings for the Second Sunday of Lent

GENESIS 22:1-2, 9A, 10-13, 15-18
"I will bless you abundantly"

PSALM 116
"I will call upon the name of the Lord"

ROMANS 8:31B-34
"If God is for us, who can be against us?"

MARK 9:2-10
"'Rabbi! It is good that we are here!"

Focus

We are transformed by the crosses of everyday life.

Opening Song (To download, visit ocp.org/renew-music.)
"Transfigure Us, O Lord," Bob Hurd

Opening Prayer

Divide the group in two, and pray alternately from Psalm 116, with everyone repeating the response:

R.   ***I will walk before the Lord, in the land of the living.***

Side 1:   *I believed, even when I said,*
                   "I am greatly afflicted."

                   Precious in the eyes of the Lord
                   Is the death of his faithful ones.

R.   ***I will walk before the Lord, in the land of the living.***

Side 2:   *O Lord, I am your servant;*
                   I am your servant, the son of your handmaid;
                   you have loosed my bonds.

                   To you will I offer sacrifice of thanksgiving.
                   and I will call upon the name of the Lord.

R.   ***I will walk before the Lord, in the land of the living.***

Side 1:   *My vows to the Lord I will pay*
                   in the presence of all his people,
                   in the courts of the house of the Lord,
                   in your midst, O Jerusalem.

R.   ***I will walk before the Lord, in the land of the living.***

The Gospel of the Lord

"Then a cloud came, casting a shadow over them; from the cloud came a voice, 'This is my beloved Son. Listen to him.' Suddenly, looking around, they no longer saw anyone but Jesus alone with them." (Mark 9:7-8)

Read *aloud Mark 9:2-10*

Reflect

What word, phrase, or image from the scripture reading touches your heart or connects to your experience?

Share with the group, or write your response here:

_____

_____

_____

_____

Old Testament Connections

Throughout the debacle of the golden calf, instigated by Aaron while Moses was in the presence of God on Sinai, Moses is sustained by a revelation of God's intimacy with him. The Hebrew people, too, draw strength from the radiance of the glory of God on the face of Moses as he returns. Put simply, Moses is a friend of God. "Thus the Lord used to speak to Moses face to face, as one speaks to a friend" (Exodus 33:11). As friendship grows, persons share with each other more of who they are. Moses shares more of his task to lead this people, and in the process, he reveals the depth of his friendship with God.

If the presence of Moses at the Transfiguration is an assurance that Jesus, too, has an intimate relationship with God's friend, the presence of Elijah is a reminder to stay the course. That Elijah was sent back out on mission even after the painful experience with King Ahab and his pagan wife, Jezebel (who vowed to stamp out worship of the Hebrew God and Elijah himself) is a message to both Jesus and the disciples. When asked by God why he has fled to Horeb, the despondent Elijah answers, "I have been very zealous for the Lord, the God of hosts; for the Israelites have forsaken your covenant, thrown down your altars, and killed your prophets with the sword. I alone am left, and they are seeking my life, to take it away (1 Kings 19:14)."

God's response is not unlike that to Moses: "Go out and stand on the mountain before the Lord, for the Lord is about to pass by." Elijah is given a commission only after he has experienced the voice of God, not in the wind, earthquake, or fire but in "a sound of sheer silence" (1 Kings 19:12).

It is often said that the Transfiguration occurred to strengthen the disciples since Jesus had just made the first prediction of his passion and death. If so, the strength is found in his intimacy with and his reliance on God in the performance of his mission. It is a message for the early Christian community: make faith in the risen Lord the central proclamation of your life—in prayer, in word, and in action.

Adapted from a reflection by Father David Reid, ss.cc., in a forthcoming book on the Gospel of Mark in the RENEW *Scripture Series.*

Reflect

The Book of Exodus says that God spoke to Moses "as one speaks to a friend," and Pope Francis has told us that "God is not a distant and anonymous being. … God is a great friend, ally, father to us, but we do not always realize it" (Angelus, February 26, 2017). How does the idea that the Creator of the universe is also your friend affect how you pray and how you live your life?

Share with the group, or write your response here.

_____

_____

_____

_____

Meditation

Fr. Bill Bausch, in his book *A World of Stories For Preachers* and Teachers, shares a scene from the musical *Man of La Mancha.* It is the story of the ridiculed Don Quixote, who lives with the illusion of being a knight of old and battles windmills that he imagines to be dragons. In one of the final scenes of the play, Don Quixote is dying with Aldonza at his side. Aldonza is thought to be a worthless whore that he had idealized, calling her Dulcinea, Sweet One—much to the amusement of the townspeople and the scorn of Aldonza herself.

But Don Quixote has loved Aldonza in a way unlike anything she has ever experienced. When Quixote breathes his last, Aldonza begins to sing "The Impossible Dream." As the last echo of the song fades away, someone shouts to her, "Aldonza!" But she stands up proudly and responds, "My name is Dulcinea." The eccentric knight's love has transformed her. For Aldonza, the moment of Quixote's death is a mountaintop experience. Quixote's spirit reflects the light of love upon her and enables her to see herself in a new light. She becomes who she really is—the Sweet One.

In the passage from Mark's Gospel, Jesus is transfigured by God the Father, reflecting divine love and light upon the apostles who witnessed the scene. Jesus becomes who he truly is—the fullest revelation of God's love and presence incarnated in the world. Peter, James, and John have gone up the mountain with Jesus, and they see him transfigured. When they come down from the mountain, he was, to appearances, the same Jesus; but they have seen him, literally, in a new light.

The three apostles themselves are not the same; they are transformed by the radiance of Christ. They are no longer ordinary fisherman but bearers of Christ's light to the world. The Transfiguration happened on the mountain but the ongoing transforming power of God's light happened to the disciples as they returned to the valley and accompanied Jesus on the way of the cross and witnessed the resurrection. I am sure the memory of the transfiguration strengthened them as they encountered their own crosses and, for Peter and James, violent deaths.

Many people have had mountaintop experiences—that is, special encounters with the Divine. These experiences can be life-changing, even miraculous, as God is revealed in new ways. God's revelation usually comes in the ordinary events of life—when God turns that which is unbearably painful into something meaningful; when God turns a joyful event into a miraculous one; when God transfigures the ordinary into a revelation of God's unconditional love for us. But the true work of transformation begins after the mountaintop, in the valley of life's difficulties, disappointments, and sufferings.

Reflect

What changed Aldonza's way of seeing herself? Who is a person who brings out the best in you?

_____

_____

_____

Describe an event or a moment in which you felt God's presence and love in a personal way? How did that experience strengthen you?

_____

_____

_____

In what way does reflecting on the sacrifice of Jesus affect your ability to deal with your own suffering and that of others?

_____

_____

_____

How has your faith in God changed your appreciation of the ordinary aspects of life?

_____

_____

_____

Jesus did not want Peter, James, and John to be preoccupied with a vision of glory before they had grasped the meaning of his death and resurrection and applied it to their life and work in the here and now. *In what ways have you experienced or witnessed new life following on death?*

_____

_____

_____

Live Lent!

✝ Think of someone who brings out the best in you. Send that person a note or an email expressing your gratitude.

✝ Affirm someone today and be conscious of and refrain from saying a negative or critical word.

† Do an act of kindness for someone who is going through a difficult time.

† Spend time prayerfully reviewing your Lenten Plan, making any adjustments that you think are needed.

 ## Closing Prayer

Pray together:

Lord God, you entered human history in the person of Jesus of Nazareth. Through Jesus, you invited us to an intimate friendship with you. We thank you for that gift and pray that the divine life that is revealed to us in him will inspire us and support us as we carry out your will each day. Help us to reflect your love to others by being kinder and more affirming to those we interact with each day.

Looking Ahead

To prepare for the next session, read the following:

- Third Sunday of Lent: Zeal for your house will consume me
- John 2:13-24

Monday

 Pray

"Deliver us and pardon our sins for your name's sake." (Psalm 79:9b)

 Read Luke 6:36-38

Summary: *"Stop judging and you will not be judged. Stop condemning and you will not be condemned. …"* (Luke 6:37a)

Spend two minutes in silence. Then repeat this passage from Scripture, and let it speak to your heart.

 Meditation

In one of his many books, twentieth-century preacher Harry Ironside repeated a story that he attributed to an Episcopal bishop of New York. According to the bishop, he had booked passage to Europe on an ocean liner, and learned when he boarded that he would be sharing a cabin with another man. After the bishop had gone to see the room, he returned to the purser's desk and asked if he could leave his gold watch and some other valuable possessions in the ship's safe. He was apologetic about making the request, but explained that he had sized up his cabin mate and thought he looked suspicious. No need to apologize, the purser said. After seeing the bishop, the other man had turned over his valuables for the same reason.

The bishop no doubt used this story to illustrate Jesus' teaching about judgment. In that teaching, as it is recorded in Luke's Gospel, Jesus was not suggesting that all actions are morally neutral, or that we should accept any kind of behavior without weighing it against the Commandments and the Gospel. In fact, statements elsewhere in Scripture, by both Jesus and St. Paul, make it clear that at times we might even be obliged to confront someone who has violated the law of God. But when Jesus said, "Stop judging and you will not be judged," he meant that we should not give ourselves credit for being more righteous than others and that we should leave the judgment of souls—our own and everyone else's—to God.

Live Lent!

I will spend time in prayer thinking of those whom I have judged harshly and perhaps have even maligned to others. I will ask God to forgive me for those judgments and give me the wisdom to avoid such judgments in the future. I will also pray that others may not judge me in the same way.

 Pray

O God, you show your love for the human race with your limitless mercy. Through your grace, may I imitate you by desiring mercy rather than condemnation. May I strive to keep myself pleasing to you and commend all others to your care. Amen.

Tuesday

 Pray

"Make justice your aim: redress the wronged, hear the orphan's plea, defend the widow." (Isaiah 1:17b)

 Read *Matthew 23:1-12*

Summary: *"The greatest among you must be your servant. Whoever exalts himself will be humbled; but whoever humbles himself will be exalted."* (Matthew 23:11-12)

Spend two minutes in silence. Then repeat this passage from Scripture, and let it speak to your heart.

![candle icon] **Meditation**

There's a story often told about George Washington that actually involved one of his generals. Jacob Francis, a soldier who enlisted in a

Massachusetts regiment during the American Revolution, reported the incident.

According to Francis, he and his fellow soldiers were building a fortification during the defense of Boston when Major General Israel Putnam rode up to observe the work. As Putnam watched, he addressed one soldier as "my lad" and told him to pick up a stone and throw it onto the middle of the fortification. The young man put his hand to his hat and told Putnam, "Sir, I am a corporal." "I ask your pardon, sir," Putnam said, and then he dismounted, threw the stone onto the breastwork himself, got back on his horse and rode off.

The lesson in humility that Putnam gave the corporal was consistent with what Jesus taught in the remarks recorded in Matthew's Gospel. Jesus didn't question the need for levels of authority in human affairs, but he did caution his followers against thinking that positions of authority made them intrinsically superior to those whom they directed. On the contrary, Jesus taught that the needs of others, and the general welfare, should take precedence over the pride of overseers—whatever form their authority might take. Whatever titles we may have—parent, teacher, supervisor, pastor, police officer—our vocation as Christians is still to serve our brothers and sisters.

Live Lent!

I will prayerfully reflect on situations in my life in which I may be in a position of authority—as an employer, a supervisor, a teacher, a grandparent or parent, or as a customer dealing with people who work in service such as waiters and waitresses, bus boys, porters, and check-out clerks. I will pray for the grace to be considerate of others in all such relationships.

 Pray

Lord Jesus, although you were God, Scripture tells us that you "emptied" yourself, taking on "the form of a slave" in order to carry out the earthly ministry that has made it possible for us to share in your divinity. Help me to remember that no matter what I achieve

or what I acquire in life, my true vocation is to imitate you by serving my brothers and sisters. Amen.

Wednesday

 Pray

"Into your hands I commend my spirit; you will redeem me, O LORD, O faithful God." *(Psalm 31:6)*

 Read *Matthew 20:17-28*

Summary: "(W)hoever wishes to be great among you shall be your servant; whoever wishes to be first among you shall be your slave. Just so, the Son of Man did not come to be served but to serve and to give his life as a ransom for many." *(Matthew 20:26b-28)*

Spend two minutes in silence. Then repeat this passage from Scripture, and let it speak to your heart.

 Meditation

Richard Parks was a professional Welsh rugby player for thirteen years until a shoulder injury forced him to retire in 2009. After his retirement, he announced that he would attempt to climb the highest mountain on each of the seven continents and stand on the North Pole, the South Pole, and the summit of Mount Everest—all within seven months. He achieved his ambition and, because his grandmother, father, and uncle had suffered from cancer, he used the self-challenge to raise the equivalent of hundreds of thousands of dollars for Madame Curie Cancer Care.

Richard Parks had this in common with the apostles James and John, the sons of Zebedee, or at least with their mother: they were ambitious. In itself, ambition is neither good nor bad. Its moral quality depends on how it is directed. Parks, no doubt frustrated by the premature end of his career, used his ambition to show that he was still capable of mighty feats. But he also applied his energy to supporting and providing publicity to an important charity. By contrast, the ambition of James and John (who, Mark's Gospel says, personally asked Jesus for the places of honor) seemed directed only at their aggrandizement.

In spite of the rebuke by Jesus the brothers continued to follow him and, after his resurrection and ascension, literally went out to teach all nations, as Jesus had commanded them. The incident we read about today was a part of their formation; they learned from it. May we apply the same lesson to ourselves by being ambitious first, not for power, prestige, or material gain, but for the wellbeing of others.

Live Lent!

I will take stock of my goals and ambitions: where I want to go, what I want to become, how I want to spend my time, what I want to acquire. Then I will commit myself to sacrificing one of these goals so that I might serve the needs of others.

 Pray

Lord Jesus Christ, you were the Son of God, and yet you set aside the glory due to you and experienced rejection, persecution, and death so that we might be gain eternal life. Help us to imitate you by preferring the common good to our personal status and comfort. Amen.

Thursday

 Pray

"For the LORD watches over the way of the just, but the way of the wicked vanishes." (Psalm 1:6)

 Read *Luke 16:19-31*

Summary: (Jesus said to the Pharisees): "There was a rich man who dressed in purple garments and fine linen and dined sumptuously each day. And lying at his door was a poor man named Lazarus, covered with sores, who would gladly have eaten his fill of the scraps that fell from the rich man's table." *(Luke 16:19-21a)*

Spend two minutes in silence. Then repeat this passage from Scripture, and let it speak to your heart.

Meditation

We usually associate Charles Dickens with Advent, not with Lent, but the central theme of his novella A Christmas Carol reflects the point Jesus made with the story of the rich man and Lazarus. In the parable, we hear the rich man futilely trying in death to intercede for the wellbeing of his living brothers after spending a lifetime thinking of no one but himself. In Dickens' story, we hear the ghost of Jacob Marley warning Ebenezer Scrooge of the fate that awaits selfish people:

``It is required of every man," Marley tells his former business partner, ``that the spirit within him should walk abroad among his fellow-men, and travel far and wide; and if that spirit goes not forth in life, it is condemned to do so after death. It is doomed to wander through the world—oh, woe is me!—and witness what it cannot share, but might have shared on earth, and turned to happiness!" Before departing, the ghost lets Scrooge momentarily glimpse the shadows of the condemned: "The misery with them all was, clearly, that they sought to interfere, for good, in human matters, and had lost the power for ever."

Pope Francis often urges us to seek out the poor and minister to them. The irony in the parable is that the rich man didn't have to "travel far and wide" to find an opportunity to relieve human misery; the opportunity lay on his doorstep. Neither would any of us have to search very far to find want, pain, or loneliness that we have the power to relieve.

Live Lent!

I will seek and take advantage of an opportunity—such as volunteering at a soup kitchen, food pantry, or nursing home—to directly help the poor.

 Pray

Father in Heaven, help me to see the many ways in which I am capable of helping the poor, and give me the will to use my gifts—time, talent, and material resources—to ease the want and suffering of my brothers and sisters. Amen.

Friday

 Pray

"Remember the marvels the Lord has done." (Psalm 105:5a)

 Read *Matthew 21:33-43, 45, 46*

Summary: *Jesus said to them, "Did you never read in the Scriptures: 'The stone that the builders rejected has become the cornerstone; by the Lord has this been done, and it is wonderful in our eyes?'"* (Matthew 21:42)

Spend two minutes in silence. Then repeat this passage from Scripture, and let it speak to your heart.

Meditation

My high school class has had several reunions since our graduation in 1960. Although many of our classmates have attended and others have at least kept in touch with us, there several from whom we have not heard in more than fifty years. No doubt this is true in part because some people are not nostalgic and are not charmed by reliving their past. Some may be ill or troubled in another way. But there were also some boys and girls who were not treated well in high school and who might not wish to be reminded of it. These were the handful of our peers who didn't fit in and were therefore abused, ridiculed, shunned, or simply ignored. We remember who those boys and girls were, and we wonder to what extent we, even by simply doing nothing, contributed to their loneliness and pain.

Rejection was a factor in the life of Jesus too. The prophet Isaiah foretold it, speaking about the Messiah who would be "despised and rejected by others" (53:3), and we read in the Gospel of John that "his own people did not accept him" (1:11). But Jesus did not reject others. In fact, he confounded the mores of his time by opening his heart to those who were routinely rejected by their community: the disabled, the destitute, lepers, tax collectors, prostitutes, Samaritans, and gentiles. If we are his disciples, we will imitate his example by offering our presence, our attention, our kindness, and our assistance to those who would otherwise be left out.

Live Lent!

I will make a conscious effort to notice anyone in my parish or in my community whom others ignore or even avoid. On my own or with my neighbors or fellow parishioners, I will try to bring some warmth and friendship to that person's life.

 Pray

Lord Jesus, you called on us to imitate you by unconditionally loving our neighbors and especially those whom no one seems to love. Give me the prudence, judgment, and greatness of heart to be a source of comfort to those who are most alone in the world. Amen.

Saturday

 Pray

"For as the heavens are high above the earth, so surpassing is his kindness toward those who fear him. As far as the east is from the

west, so far has he put our transgressions from us." (Psalm 103:11-12)

 Read *Luke 15:1-3, 11-32*

Summary: *"(N)ow we must celebrate and rejoice, because your brother was dead and has come to life again; he was lost and has been found."* (Luke 15:32)

Spend two minutes in silence. Then repeat this passage from Scripture, and let it speak to your heart.

Meditation

Roy Riegels wasn't 20 years old, but he felt as if life was over. Riegels played center for the University of California, Berkeley, in the 1929 Rose Bowl Game against Georgia Tech. In the second quarter, Riegels retrieved a Tech fumble about thirty yards from his team's end zone, but in the confusion, he ran sixty-nine yards in the wrong direction until he was stopped at Cal's one-yard line. Tech eventually scored on a safety and won the game. In the clubhouse, Riegels sat alone and wept, but coach Nibs Price announced that the same team that started the game would start the second half. "I can't do it," Riegels told him. "I've ruined you. I've ruined myself. … I couldn't face that crowd to save my life." But Price told him to get out on the field. Riegels did play, and he played well. He was team captain and an All-American the following season. In later life, he taught, coached scholastic football, served in the Army Air Corps, and was a respected businessman.

Nibs Price had watched Riegels commit perhaps the biggest blunder in collegiate football but, even with the Rose Bowl Game and his own reputation on the line, he gave the young man a second chance. The parable of the father and his sons is about second chances. Jesus is about second chances. God, who prefers mercy to punishment, is about second chances—or as many chances as it takes. And Lent is an opportunity for us to turn to God, acknowledge the ways in which we haven't fully lived the Gospel and, with his blessing, begin again.

Live Lent!

I will receive the sacrament of reconciliation and resolve to extend to others the patience and mercy God has shown to me.

 Pray

Merciful God, when I open my heart to you like the young man of the parable returning to his father, accept my penance and my determination to renew my life and to joyfully share my peace with the world. Amen.

Third Sunday of Lent

Zeal for your house will consume me.

Suggested Environment

A small table with a burning candle and a Bible opened to the gospel reading for this session. Consider decorating the table with violet, the liturgical color of the Lenten season. Scatter some coins across the table to evoke the image in today's Gospel reading—money-changers in the Temple.

Liturgical Readings for the Third Sunday of Lent

EXODUS 20:1-17
"You shall not have other gods besides me."

PSALM 19:8,9,10,11
"The ordinances of the Lord are true, all of them just."

1 CORINTHIANS 1:22-25
"The foolishness of God is wiser than human wisdom."

JOHN 2:13-25
"Stop making my Father's house a marketplace."

Focus

It's time to clean house.

Opening Song (To download, visit ocp.org/renew-music.)
"Change Our Hearts," Rory Cooney

✝ **Opening Prayer**

Divide the group in two, and pray alternately from Psalm 19, with everyone repeating the response.

R.   **Lord, you have the words of everlasting life.**

Side 1:   *The law of the Lord is perfect,*
             refreshing the soul.

             The decree of the Lord is trustworthy,
             giving wisdom to the simple.

R.   **Lord, you have the words of everlasting life.**

Side 2:   *The precepts of the Lord are right,*
             rejoicing the heart.

             The command of the Lord is clear,
             enlightening the eye.

R.   **Lord, you have the words of everlasting life.**

Side 1:   *The fear of the Lord is pure,*
             enduring forever.

             The ordinances of the Lord are true,
             all of them just.

R.   **Lord, you have the words of everlasting life.**

Side 2:   *They are more precious than gold,*
             than a heap of purest gold;
             sweeter also than syrup
             or honey from the comb.

R.   **Lord, you have the words of everlasting life.**

All: **Amen.**

⊕ The Gospel of the Lord

"He told those who were selling the doves, 'Take these things out of here! Stop making my Father's house a marketplace!' His disciples remembered that it is written, 'Zeal for your house will consume me.'"
(John 2:16-17)

Read aloud John 2:13-24

Reflect

What word, phrase of image from the Gospel reading touches your heart or connects to your experience. Share with your group, and/or write your response here:

_____

_____

_____

_____

Old Testament Connections

John uses words from Psalm 69 to anchor the phrase "zeal for the house of the Lord will consume me" as the pivotal Old Testament text for his teaching about the Temple-cleansing incident. The passage from Psalm 69 states that zeal for the house of God makes the writer of the psalm vulnerable to the scorn and abuse of others (69:9).

Matthew, Mark and Luke all use a different passage from the Old Testament—from the firebrand prophet Jeremiah (7:9-15). Jeremiah upbraids the people of Israel for violating God's commandments in both their treatment of each other and in their practice of pagan rituals. He reminds his people they had another shrine to the Lord at Shiloh (in the North) and that the Lord will do to their Temple in Jerusalem what he did to Shiloh: permit its destruction. And, indeed, it happened in the sixth century B.C. So, Matthew, Mark, and Luke use this reference to reflect on the destruction of the Jerusalem Temple in their time, around 70 A.D.

John takes a new tack. There are no more Temples made of stone. There is an entirely new Temple, not made with human hands. It is the Temple of God found in the person of Jesus. And zeal for this Temple should consume us. It is a positive and a defining message with an entirely new image: Christ with us!

Adapted from a reflection by Martin Lang in John: I Am the Vine, *part of the* RENEW Scripture Series.

Reflect

The destruction of the Jerusalem Temple was a devastating experience for the Jewish people. They thought that without the Temple they could not experience the presence of God. How do you experience God's presence when you visit a church or attend Mass? Are there other places where you particularly feel the presence of God?

The reflection says that zeal for the person of Jesus, present in our lives, should consume us? In what ways do you experience this in your daily life? What can you do to increase your zeal for God this Lent?

Share with the group, and/or write your response here.

_____

_____

_____

_____

 Meditation

Many years ago, I met a faith-filled family that owned a dry-cleaning business. Their founding store, started by their immigrant grandparents, was in Brooklyn. The grandparents toiled every day to build the business to support their family. The next generation developed a couple of dry-cleaning stores in the suburbs, but the heart of their family business remained in Brooklyn. Photos of their grandparents, parents, aunts and uncles working the 20th century steam presses papered the walls.

One night, a fast-moving, six-alarm fire tore through several buildings on the street where the original store was located. When Tony, a grandson of the founders, arrived at the scene with his family, they encountered smoke, water, and broken glass. More than 200 firefighters battled the flames in what turned out to be a devastating night for business owners and residents. In the end, when Tony looked at his corner store, there was only a burned-out shell of charred wood and a blue sky above.

Tony and his family were distraught. The legacy of their grandparents had been destroyed. Tony's brother and sister began to weep. After regaining his composure, Tony began to gather material to make a sign. He carried the sign to the middle of the rubble and planted it. It read: "Thank God we are all alive!"

This simple hand-painted sign was a tremendous witness to faith and hope for the family as well as the neighbors. The heart of the business was not the building but Tony's grandparents and parents who had toiled under difficult conditions, working 12 hours a day, to make a better life for their family. Tony reminded his family: Their spirit and legacy is not confined to a building but lives on in us, and thank God we are alive to carry it forward.

In the gospel passage about the cleansing of the temple in Jerusalem, we encounter a passionate and zealous Jesus as he drives out the merchants. His actions recall for the disciples the scripture verse, "Zeal for your house consumes me." Jesus wasn't interested in redecorating the temple or simply purging the temple of business dealings; his zeal was for purifying the community of believers and restoring their awareness of his sacred presence. He overturned the table of the money changers, and all turned to chaos. "Overturned" is a key word, because Jesus turned upside-down much of what was thought to be authentic and appropriate worship. His actions reveal that true worship is found in the new temple of God found in the person of Jesus the Christ.

The Church in our time needs reform and purification. Pope Francis continues to "overturn"—turn upside-down—some of the lax and self-serving structures and corrupt practices that have become entrenched in the Vatican. A couple of years ago, in a Christmas address to an audience of surprised cardinals, he began by denouncing the various "diseases" of the Curia—its "pathology of power," its "rivalry and vainglory," its "gossiping, grumbling and backbiting," its "careerism and opportunism." He continues to challenge the Church throughout the world to become more poor and for the poor, to root out clericalism, and to be focused on service and mercy.

We also need reform and purification. St. Paul reminds us that as followers of Jesus Christ we are temples of the Holy Spirit—dwelling places of God. We too become lax in our faith, self-serving and more concerned about outward appearances. What in your life needs to be overturned and set right? Do you have your priorities straight? Are you engaged in back biting and gossip?

God's power is not revealed in fancy clothes or in magnificent stones but rather in the broken and pierced body of Jesus Christ. Our physical body will pass away, but our spirits will live forever. Thank God we are alive and can ask God again for the grace to put our house back in order and live more authentic lives of love and mercy.

Reflect

What touched you about the story of the dry-cleaning business? What did you learn from this story that you can apply to your life?

_____

_____

_____

_____

In what ways do you experience, in yourself or others, the ills that Pope Francis has identified in the hierarchy of the Church—such things as rivalry, gossiping, grumbling, and opportunism? What are the remedies for these "diseases"?

_____

_____

_____

_____

St. Paul made a challenging statement when he wrote that, as followers of Christ, we are temples of the Holy Spirit. What thoughts does his statement inspire in you?

_____

_____

_____

_____

Live Lent!

Reflect on each of the ills that Pope Francis challenges us to resist. Identify one that you most need to deal with. Make a commitment to do one thing this week that will help you eliminate one of these bad habits.

† Each day this week spend time thanking God for your life and all your blessings.

† Those who are poor suffer the most from injustice—such as the short-changing and over-charging practiced by the merchants in the Temple—and from insensitivity or poor priorities in public policy. Catholic Relief Services, one of the largest charitable organizations in the world, works to raise those who are poor to greater independence. Research the work CRS is doing throughout the planet, (www.crs.org, www.confrontglobalpoverty.org). Decide how you can best support this work and help others to learn about it.

† Spend time prayerfully reviewing your Lenten Plan, making any adjustments that you think are needed.

✝ Closing Prayer

Pray together:

Gracious God, thank you for the gift of life and for always giving me another chance to be forgiven and renewed in faith. Help me to clean my own house this Lent and set my priorities according to your will. Renew the Church, focus us beyond ourselves, and help us become more powerful witnesses of peace, justice and authenticity.

Looking Ahead

To prepare for the next session, read the following:

- Fourth Sunday of Lent: Come to the light
- John 3:14-21

Monday

 Pray

"A thirst is my soul for God, the living God. When shall I go and behold the face of God?" (Psalm 42:2)

 Read Luke 4:24-30

Summary: (Jesus said to the people in the synagogue at Nazareth) "Again, there were many lepers in Israel during the time of Elisha the prophet; yet not one of them was cleansed, but only Naaman the Syrian." When the people in the synagogue heard this, they were all filled with fury." (Luke 4:27-28)

Spend two minutes in silence. Then repeat this passage from Scripture, and let it speak to your heart.

 Meditation

When I was editor of a daily newspaper, we periodically invited about a dozen readers to discuss the newspaper and the community. At one such gathering, I distributed copies of a weekly Spanish-language newspaper that we also published. One woman angrily asked why we, as she put it, encouraged people to use Spanish instead of learning English—a complaint that often masks a deeper resentment of immigrants. I explained that the weekly served the needs of recent immigrants who had not yet mastered English, and that many others who read the weekly also read our English daily. She was not sympathetic.

Later, when the subject had changed, the same woman said with a laugh, "My mother came here from Greece sixty years ago, and she still doesn't speak a word of English!"

The Old and New Testaments confirm that antagonism toward people from other cultures is nothing new. When Jesus told his neighbors in small, insular Nazareth that foreigners might be more likely than they to accept his teaching, their reaction was violent, but not unfamiliar.

In our own time, global communications can promote understanding among people of different beliefs and backgrounds; unfortunately, however, this technology has also demonstrated its power to broadcast stereotypes and fan paranoia and hatred. We disciples of Jesus are called to be more thoughtful, to see in faces of every description the face of God. As Pope Francis has reminded us, we are called to "listen to one another, to make plans together, and in this way to overcome suspicion and prejudice, and to build a coexistence that is ever more secure, peaceful, and inclusive" (Angelus, November 16, 2014).

Live Lent!

I will make a point of being open-minded and welcoming whenever and wherever I meet people whose ethnic or religious backgrounds are different from my own.

 Pray

Creator God, our world, which exists only because of your will, is adorned with diversity. Give me the freedom of spirit to rejoice in the diversity among my fellow human beings and to treat people of every description with dignity and appreciation. Amen.

Tuesday

 Pray

"He guides the humble to justice, he teaches the humble his way." (Psalm 25:9)

 Read *Matthew 18:21-35*

Summary: "His master summoned him and said to him, 'You wicked servant! I forgave you your entire debt

because you begged me to. Should you not have had pity on your fellow servant, as I had pity on you?'"
(Matthew 18:32-33)

Spend two minutes in silence. Then repeat this passage from Scripture, and let it speak to your heart.

 **Meditation**

In April 1830 George Wilson and James Porter were charged with robbing the mail and assaulting a mail driver in Pennsylvania. Both men pleaded not guilty, and Porter was put to death. Wilson later changed his plea to guilty. There were multiple sentences in the case. In June of that year, President Andrew Jackson pardoned Wilson with respect to the death penalty, but Wilson—without explaining himself—declined the pardon. Through a complicated legal process, the U.S. Supreme Court in 1833 considered the odd question of whether Wilson, or any convicted person, can reject a pardon. Chief Justice John Marshall, describing a pardon as "an act of grace," wrote, "It may ... be rejected by the person to whom it is tendered, ... we have discovered no power in a court to force it on him."

The parable of the unforgiving servant is another story of pardon granted and rejected. No doubt, the servant was glad that the king had forgiven a large debt. Who wouldn't be? But the king's mercy did not touch the servant's heart; it did not inspire an interior conversion in him. Although the king later withdrew his pardon, it was really the mean-spirited servant who rejected it by proving himself unworthy.

God has promised to forgive our sins if we repent, but repentance doesn't mean only a sigh of relief. The word implies a turning, away from sin and toward a better life—in other words, a conversion. Accepting God's pardon means resolving to change our lives.

Live Lent!

I will examine my conscience and make a sincere Act of Contrition; I will rejoice in the ways my renewed spirit affects the routine business of my life today.

Pray

O God in Heaven, you are mercy itself. I acknowledge to you my failings and I pledge to you that the grace of your forgiveness will radiate from me to warm the lives of everyone I meet. Amen.

Wednesday

 Pray

"He sends forth his command to the earth; swiftly runs his word!"
(Psalm 147:15)

Read Matthew 5:17-19

Summary: *"Amen, I say to you, until heaven and earth pass away, not the smallest letter or the smallest part of a letter will pass from the law, ..."* (Matthew 5:18)

Spend two minutes in silence. Then repeat this passage from Scripture, and let it speak to your heart.

Meditation

On December 1, 1955, Rosa Parks boarded a bus in Montgomery, Alabama, and sat in the eleventh row of seats. Under a Montgomery ordinance, the first ten rows on a city bus were reserved for white people. But the bus was crowded, and the driver told Mrs. Parks that she would have to move to make room for white passengers. Mrs. Parks refused, arguing that she was acting within the law, but the driver argued that the law empowered him to separate white and black passengers. The driver called the police, Mrs. Parks was arrested, and the incident sparked the historic Montgomery bus boycott.

While Mrs. Parks' conviction was being appealed, a U.S. District Court and then the U.S. Supreme Court ruled that the Montgomery city law was no law at all—it was unconstitutional.

Rosa Parks' experience dramatized the principle that law does not exist so that stronger people can oppress weaker people. That's why the Montgomery law was no law at all. When Jesus said the smallest detail of the law would remain in place he was not referring to the myriad of dietary and purity regulations that had been imposed on the Jewish people over several generations. He was referring to the law imparted through Moses and summarized in the Ten Commandments: the law that teaches us to indiscriminately love one another as God has loved us.

Jesus criticized pointless regulations that weighed people down and did nothing to help them, but he upheld the law that is written in our hearts—the law we obey not out of fear but out of love.

Live Lent!

I will be conscious of how I live the Gospel in my observance of such things as speed limits and environmental regulations that are designed to protect the common good.

 Pray

Loving God, your law teaches us to care for each other and for the world in which we live. Help me to apply that law to every decision I make and every action I take in my daily life. Amen.

Thursday

 Pray

"Come, let us bow down in worship; let us kneel before the LORD who made us. For he is our God, and we are the people he shepherds, the flock he guides." (Psalm 95, 6-7)

 Read *Luke 11:14-23*

Summary: *"(I)f it is by the finger of God that I drive out demons, then the Kingdom of God has come upon you." (Luke 11:20)*

Spend two minutes in silence. Then repeat this passage from Scripture, and let it speak to your heart.

 Meditation

In 1954, William Golding published a novel about a group of boys marooned on a remote Pacific island. In this story, Golding related how the boys' little society deteriorated into chaos as their worst instincts overwhelmed any sense of a common good. The inner demon that stifled the boys' better nature is known euphemistically as "the lord of the flies," and that provided the title of the novel. "The lord of the flies," in turn, is a translation of "Beelzebul," the name used by Jesus and his critics to refer to the devil.

Some of the folks who saw Jesus rid the speechless man of a demon could not rejoice in the fact that their neighbor had been made whole; instead, they let their own inner demons take over as they challenged Jesus, insisting that his power to heal must come from an evil source. This impulse to be cynical and self-centered, and to disregard the wellbeing of our neighbor, can arise at any time in everyday life.

We may not recognize Beelzebul, but he's lurking nearby when we engage in destructive gossip; when we speed or cut off other drivers so that we can be first by a few seconds; when we are rude to service people such as waiters, cashiers, or gas station attendants; or when we use hurtful language to contradict or belittle family members, co-workers, or friends. But this impulse can be checked by a life of prayer in which we are in constant conversation with our Savior. When we invite the companionship of Jesus, we keep the lord of the flies at bay.

Live Lent!

I will take the time to review my day and ask myself when I thought of my own benefit instead of the welfare of others. If there were such times, I will pray for forgiveness. If there were no such times, I will thank God for his grace.

Pray

Loving God, I know that you are present everywhere and at all times. I pray that everything I think, say, and do each day will be blessed by my awareness of your presence. Be close to me always in the person of your son, Jesus Christ. Amen.

Friday

 Pray

"There shall be no strange god among you nor shall you worship any alien god." (Psalm 81:10)

 Read *Mark 12:28-34*

Summary: *"One of the scribes came to Jesus and asked him, 'Which is the first of all the commandments?' Jesus replied, 'The first is this: Hear, O Israel! The Lord our God is Lord alone! You shall love the Lord your God with all your heart, with all your soul, with all your mind, and with all your strength.'"* (Mark 12:28-30)

Spend two minutes in silence. Then repeat this passage from Scripture, and let it speak to your heart.

 Meditation

I once read a blog post in which a priest told of a frivolous contest run by a radio station. Listeners to the station, which was at FM frequency 106, were invited to set their clock radios to that station and, when they got up in the morning, call and report the first words they had said that day. The third caller each day would win $106. Responses included "Do I smell coffee burning?" and "Honey, did I put the dog out last night?" But one morning the third caller said something unexpected. His first words had been, "Hear, O Israel, the Lord our God, the Lord is one. ..."

That man had begun the day by saying the prayer known in Hebrew as Shema Yisrael, which is taken from the Book of Deuteronomy 6:4-9. This declaration of the oneness of God is so important in Jewish tradition that when Jesus was asked what was first among the commandments, he did not refer to the Decalogue but to the Shema. Observant Jews recite this prayer the first thing in the morning and the last thing at night, they teach it to their children, and they hope it will be last words they say before dying. It is part of a tradition in which prayer is a central component of everyday life.

The man who called the radio station provided a good example to all believers. Beginning the day by acknowledging God is a good start to keeping God at the forefront of our thoughts during the activities of our daily lives. Even the simplest prayer in the morning can lead to a whole day dedicated to the one God, and to none of the other "gods" that can preoccupy us.

Live Lent!

I will begin during this season to develop the habit of acknowledging God with praise and gratitude at the beginning of each day of my life.

 Pray

All-powerful God, I thank you for the gift of each day of my life. Give me the grace to make each day, even in its simplest details, a sign of my love for you and my gratitude for your love. Amen.

Saturday

 Pray

"Have mercy on me, O God, in your goodness; in the greatness of your compassion wipe out my offense." (Psalm 51:3)

Read *Luke 18:9-14*

Summary: *"But the tax collector stood off at a distance and*

would not even raise his eyes to heaven but beat
his breast and prayed, 'O God, be merciful to me a
sinner.'" (Luke 18:13)

Spend two minutes in silence. Then repeat this passage from Scripture, and let it speak to your heart.

 ## Meditation

The parable of the tax collector and the Pharisee calls to mind a story that is usually attributed to Frederick II, also called "the Great," who was king of Prussia for more than forty years in the 18th century. The story goes that Frederick visited a prison and spoke with several of the inmates. One after another, the inmates told the king that they were imprisoned unjustly. Frederick approached one man by saying, "And you. I suppose you're innocent too?" "No, majesty," the man said. "I'm guilty, and I deserve to be punished." Frederick then turned to the jailer and said, "Release this man. I don't want him corrupting all these innocent victims!"

Our Christian faith is not about guilt but about mercy. But in order to be in a right relationship with God, we must acknowledge our mistakes as that last prisoner did, sincerely commit ourselves to avoid them in the future, and ask for the forgiveness that God has promised us. When we have repented and received God's grace, our previous failings need no longer weigh us down.

The Pharisee is convinced of the human failings of the tax collector but cannot admit to the weaknesses he himself certainly has. He stands in the way of his own salvation. The tax collector, on the other hand, knows who he is and knows that he must—and can—be reconciled with God. When he has done that, his sins will be as nothing. At the moment described in Jesus' story, the tax collector experiences a "little Lent," and he gives us a model to imitate during this holy season.

Live Lent!

I will consider adopting the "Examen of Consciousness" of St. Ignatius Loyola as a daily exercise (see http://www.ignatianspirituality.com/

ignatian-prayer/the-examen). I will review my daily life for the past week and make an Act of Contrition.

 Pray

O God, the prophets and the psalms spoke of your mercy. Jesus, your Son, proclaimed it in his teaching and practiced it in his ministry. I submit to you all of my human failings, confident that you extend your mercy to me, accept my penitence, and embrace me as your loved one. Amen.

Fourth Sunday of Lent

Come to the light

Suggested Environment

A small table with a burning candle, a crucifix, and a Bible opened to the gospel reading for this session. Consider decorating the table with violet, the liturgical color of the Lenten season, or rose, the liturgical color of this Sunday—known as Laetare Sunday. This Sunday gets its name from the first words of the traditional entrance antiphon for the Mass of the day, "Laetare, Jerusalem" ("Rejoice, Jerusalem"). We rejoice in the midst of the solemn season of Lent, because we anticipate the Easter celebration of our salvation.

Liturgical Readings for the
Fourth Sunday of Lent

2 CHRONICLES 36:14-16, 19-23
God's people redeemed from Babylon

PSALM 137:1-2,3,4-5
"May I never forget Jerusalem"

EPHESIANS 2:4-10
"By grace you have been saved"

JOHN 3:14-21
"The Son of Man must be lifted up"

Focus

If we accept Christ, we will have eternal life.

Opening Song (To download, visit ocp.org/renew-music.)
"Christ, Be Our Light," Bernadette Farrell

Opening Prayer

Divide the group in two, and pray together from Psalm 137, with everyone repeating the response:

R.   ***Let my tongue be silenced if I ever forget you!***

Side 1:   *By the streams of Babylon*
                we sat and wept
                when we remembered Zion.

                On the aspens of that land
                we hung up our harps.

R.   ***Let my tongue be silenced if I ever forget you!***

Side 2:   *For there our captors asked of us*
                the lyrics of our songs,

                and our despoilers urged us to be joyous:
                "Sing for us the songs of Zion!"

R.   ***Let my tongue be silenced if I ever forget you!***

Side 1:   *How could we sing a song of the Lord*
                in a foreign land?

                If I forget you, Jerusalem,
                May my right hand be forgotten!

R.   ***Let my tongue be silenced if I ever forget you!***

Side 2:   *OMay my tongue cleave to my palate*
                if I remember you not,

                if I place not Jerusalem
                ahead of my joy.

The Gospel of the Lord

"For God so loved the world that he gave his only Son, so that everyone who believes in him might not perish but might have eternal life. For God did not send his Son into the world to condemn the world, but that the world might be saved through him." (John 3:16).

Read aloud John 3:14-21

Reflect

What word, phrase, or image from the scripture reading touches your heart or connects to your experience?

Share with the group, or write your response here:

_____

_____

_____

_____

Old Testament Connections

"Just as Moses lifted up the serpent in the wilderness, so must the Son of Man be lifted up." Moses stood, both hands fully extended in a "V-like" stance, holding aloft his walking stick. A bronze snake was wound around the stick. As long as Moses stood in this position those of his people who were bitten by the desert-dwelling serpents would be saved from death (Numbers 21:8). Moses in this vision is a saving leader; his outstretched arms protect his people. The Son of Man, similarly outstretched upon the cross, endures far more suffering than did Moses. We are encouraged to look upon the Son of Man in this crucified image. It is the age-old symbol of Christian belief: Jesus the savior of the world. "Whoever believes in him (will) have eternal life."

"God so loved the world that he gave his only Son, so that everyone who believes in him may not perish but may have eternal life." The "world" in John's Gospel is not the bluish-green orb that astronauts see. It is a complex of values unworthy of our life-commitment. There is a dichotomy between the values of the world and those taught by Jesus. Yet in this passage we are told that the Son did not come to condemn the world but to shed light on it—that is, to expose its values so that people can commit to a new vision, a lifetime of supporting the values of the divine intent.

Prophets of the Old Testament often denounce sin and sinners. They reflect the view that the consequence of sin is death. We do not see that here. This Gospel is different. Turning to Jesus does not mean being steeped in recalling of past sins. It consists of recognizing signs and symbols, new images given to us, such as coming from darkness into the light, looking upon the one pierced or being born again, emerging from the waters as a new creation. It is about a God who offers us his only Son, Jesus, because "God so loves the world"— emphasis on the gift, emphasis on a loving and a generous God. The first step in this newly revealed spirituality is an appreciation for this divine generosity.

Adapted from a reflection by Martin Lang in John: I Am the Vine, *part of the* RENEW Scripture Series.

Reflect

The cross is a symbol of Christian faith. Share about a cross or crucifix that has particular meaning to you.

Share with the group, and/or write your response here.

_____

_____

_____

_____

Meditation

In the 1970's the biblical verse John 3:16 began appearing at sport stadiums: "For God so loved the world that he gave his only Son, so that everyone who believes in him may not perish but may have eternal life." It was a way for evangelical Christians to witness to their faith on a national platform. In 2009, the verse was propelled back into the news when Tim Tebow, the University of Florida quarterback, wore eye black (grease under a player's eye that reduces sun glare) with the inscription

"John 3:16" as he led the Gators over the University of Oklahoma Sooners to a national college championship. It was reported that 94 million sports fans Googled "John 3:16" during the game—it was the No. 1 hot trend search.

This verse and today's whole gospel passage is part of Jesus' remarks to the Pharisee Nicodemus, who came to Jesus under cover of night. Earlier in this discourse, Jesus told Nicodemus, "No one can see the kingdom of God without being born from above" (verse 3:3). This is the verse most often chosen to witness to Christ, and it has become a rallying cry for a segment of contemporary North American Christianity—you must be "born again." The popular understanding of "born again" emphasizes personal conversion sometimes to the exclusion of the source of that change, which is the cross of Christ. The radical new life we receive in Christ is a life born of water and spirit—a life regenerated through Jesus' offer of his own life. To be born from above is to be born again through the "lifting up" and "exalting" of Jesus on the cross. This is both a personal and communal experience.

As Catholics, we understand being "born again" as rooted in our baptism which invites us to ongoing conversion to Christ. Claiming our personal belief in Christ changes our lives so that we can speak of being born again because of the new life that comes with an awareness of the full character of God that is revealed in Jesus. To believe in Jesus is to believe that God gives his Son in love as a gift to all people to bring healing and new life to a suffering and broken world. It is up to each person to accept the gift through God's grace and with the support of the community of the faithful, the Church.

Today's passage tells us that if we accept Christ we will have eternal life. "Eternal life" is one of the key themes in the Gospel of John. For John, "eternal life" does not mean merely the endless duration of human existence but living in the unending presence of God, beginning now.

This chapter of John's Gospel invites us to enter into the conversation between Jesus and Nicodemus. Jesus asks Nicodemus, a teacher of the Torah, to let go of certitude in order to be born anew to the life Jesus is offering him. Nicodemus' night visit is exploratory; he is a seeker, and in the gospel account Nicodemus does not understand what Jesus is inviting him to. Nicodemus struggles with the literal meaning of being born again and thus remains in the dark. As with Nicodemus, our assumptions and certitudes sometimes block us from a fuller experience of God. This Lent is an opportunity to let go of certitudes, and allow the light of God's love to shine on your present reality—on the people, places and situations that are calling you to be the presence of God.

Reflect

Has anyone asked you if you were born again? What did it mean to you, or how did you answer the question? How would you answer the question if it were posed tonight?

_____

_____

_____

_____

Eternal life is a key metaphor in the Gospel of John. *How do you relate to "eternal life" as living in the unending presence of God?*

_____

_____

_____

_____

How do some of your certitudes and assumptions block you from experiencing the fullness of God in situations? In yourself? In others? Can you name an experience of letting go of what you thought you knew?

_____

_____

_____

_____

Live Lent!

† Buy a cross and hang it on a wall in your home.

† Name a certitude or assumption that you hold that has caused you to shut someone out of your life or caused you to judge a person or group of persons harshly. Bring it to your conversation with Christ, and ask him to shine his light.

† Spend time prayerfully reviewing your Lenten Plan, making any adjustments that you think are needed.

✝ Closing Prayer

Pray together:

Loving God, we thank you for giving Jesus in love to all people. Your great love, that knows no bounds, gives life to faith. Give us the grace to accept the gift of Jesus into our hearts so we may be born anew. Thank you for the gift of eternal life that begins now as we say yes to walking with Christ each day and living in the unending presence of God. Amen.

Looking Ahead

To prepare for the next session, read the following:

- Fifth Sunday of Lent: The passion foretold
- John 12:20-33

Monday

 Pray

"Sing praise to the LORD, you his faithful ones, and give thanks to his holy name. For his anger lasts but a moment; a lifetime, his good will." (Psalm 30:5-6a)

 Read *John 4:43-54*

Summary: *"They told him, 'The fever left him yesterday, about one in the afternoon.' The father realized that just at that time Jesus had said to him, 'Your son will live,' and he and his whole household came to believe." (John 4:52b-53)*

Spend two minutes in silence. Then repeat this passage from Scripture, and let it speak to your heart.

 Meditation

In the 1977 movie *Oh, God!*, the Almighty, played by George Burns, recruits Jerry Landers, played by John Denver, to become a prophet to the modern world. The movie, a $51-million-dollar hit, was light on substance and heavy on platitudes. Many religious groups criticized it as sacrilegious.

In a broad way, the movie evoked the experience of Moses who balked when God proposed to speak through him. Moses objected that he was not eloquent enough to confront Pharaoh and demand the liberation of the Hebrews. And Jerry Landers argued—correctly, as it turned out—that people wouldn't listen to him. At one point, "God" responded to this doubt by saying, "Trust me—like it says on the money."

Whatever the shortcomings of the movie, that one line was good advice. We see the idea presented more sublimely in the account of the royal official who asked Jesus to help a son who was near death. There are conflicting opinions as to whether Jesus was addressing this official or curious bystanders with the remark, "Unless you people see signs and wonders, you will not believe." But when Jesus told the official, "You may go; your son will live," the official trusted him and set off for home.

This is an important example for us during Lent—not because we may be asking God to heal us physically, but because we are asking him to heal us spiritually. It's easy to become discouraged by our mistakes, but God has promised us that if we sincerely repent, he will forgive us anything. So we can approach our Lenten practices not with trepidation but with confidence because, after all, in God we trust.

Live Lent!

I will focus my attention on the habit or mistake that plagues me most often. I will pray for the fortitude to avoid this problem in the future, thank God for forgiving my sins in the past, and dismiss any doubt that God will be with me as I continue my spiritual journey.

 Pray

O forgiving God, you know better than I do the missteps in my life. I am truly sorry for all of these. I am determined to live in keeping with the Gospel, and I trust in your promise to love me as I am, lift me up when I fall, and embrace me at the end of my life's journey. Amen.

Tuesday

 Pray

"God is our refuge and our strength, an ever-present help in distress." (Psalm 46:1)

 Read *John 5:1-16*

Summary: *"Look, you are well; do not sin any more, so that nothing worse may happen to you."* (John 5:14b)

Spend two minutes in silence. Then repeat this passage from Scripture, and let it speak to your heart.

Meditation

Joseph approached me before the third meeting of a college class and asked if I would let him in. He had failed the course once, he said, although the instructor had admired his work. I let him join; he didn't complete one assignment. But that was the fault of the friend who borrowed Joe's laptop, the stranger who took Joe's briefcase, the pal who needed a ride out of state—anyone but Joe.

Joe comes to mind in light of the cure of the paralyzed man. Although a disabled man is a sympathetic figure, this one was reluctant to take responsibility for himself. When Jesus asked if he wanted to be healed, the man didn't shout "yes"; instead, he made excuses for why he hadn't been healed before. People wouldn't help him; it was their fault. When folks asked the man why he was carrying his mat on the Sabbath, he didn't say he had just been cured of paralysis and was happy just to be able to stand. Instead, he said that "the man"—he hadn't thought to ask Jesus' name—had told him to carry it. It was "the man's" fault. And in their second encounter, Jesus' implied that he knew that many of the cured fellow's problems were of his own making.

Joseph and the paralytic man aren't unusual in putting the blame on others. But Lent is an opportunity to be honest, with God and with ourselves, and to acknowledge the failings that we are responsible for—not so that we can feel the embarrassment we've been trying to avoid, but so that we can start life anew knowing that God forgives us.

Live Lent!

I will think about my life and single out one way in which I could be a better person—healthier, more productive, more patient, more generous—and in which, through my own fault, I have not grown. Perhaps it is the problem I identified during yesterday's reflection; perhaps it is something else. I will resolve to act upon this one aspect of my life, and I will pray to God for the grace to persevere.

Pray

Merciful God, like Eve who blamed the serpent for her sin, and like Adam who blamed Eve, I may try at times to avoid responsibility for my actions. But you know me better than I know myself, and so I pray for the courage to acknowledge my mistakes so that I can avoid them in the future and grow ever closer to you. Amen.

Wednesday

 Pray

"The Lord is gracious and merciful, slow to anger and of great kindness. The Lord is good to all and compassionate toward all his works." (Psalm 145:8-9)

 Read *John 5:17-30*

Summary: "Whoever does not honor the Son does not honor the Father who sent him. Amen, amen, I say to you, whoever hears my word and believes in the one who sent me has eternal life and will not come to condemnation, but has passed from death to life." (John 5: 23b-24)

Spend two minutes in silence. Then repeat this passage from Scripture, and let it speak to your heart.

 Meditation

The author Salman Rushdie once described Dan Brown's *The Da Vinci Code* as "a novel so bad that it gives bad novels a bad name." Not all critics agreed when the book was published in 2003, and—good or bad—Brown's tale was one of the two top-selling books that year. But the Church and many Christians found the book offensive, with its premise that Jesus had married Mary Magdalene and fathered children with her, and with its implication that the notion that Jesus was both human and divine was fabricated in order to make Christianity more palatable to pagans who were accustomed to worshiping demigods.

Dan Brown was not the first, nor will he be the last, to challenge the central tenet of our faith: that Jesus has both the nature of humanity and the nature of God, and that in his divine nature he is one in the Trinity with the Father and the Holy Spirit. But we Christians reflect on the teachings of Jesus, not only because they show us the only path to peace and justice on earth but also because Jesus spoke with the authority of God.

During Lent, as we re-form our lives to bring them even more in tune with the values of the Gospel, we should not approach it as a self-help exercise. We should approach it as an encounter with the person, Jesus, who is the tangible sign of God's presence in the world and of God's inexhaustible love for us.

Live Lent!

I will prayerfully read some stories of the compassion of Jesus, remembering that this compassion, which is the will of God, envelops me even in my imperfection. (See, for example, Luke 7:11-17; Luke 7:36-50; and John 8:3-11.)

 Pray

Loving God, in the person of Jesus you made possible for us an intimate relationship with you in the visible, tangible world. Help us to imitate Jesus by conforming our will to your will and to recognize in his love and mercy the grace that comes from your own infinite generosity. Amen.

Thursday

 Pray

"They forgot the God who had saved them, who had done great

---

deeds in Egypt ..." (Psalm 106:21)

 Read *John 5:31-47*

Summary: *"I came in the name of my Father, but you do not accept me; yet if another comes in his own name, you will accept him."* (John 5:43)

Spend two minutes in silence. Then repeat this passage from Scripture, and let it speak to your heart.

 Meditation

An acquaintance of mine is absorbed in the divine forces in nature, spiritual healing, and figures like the Dalai Lama. She posted on a social media site this statement by the Buddhist sage: "It is far more useful to be aware of a single shortcoming in ourselves than it is to be aware of a thousand in somebody else." I answered with a statement by Jesus recorded in the Gospel according to Luke: "How can you say, 'Let me remove the speck from your eye' when you cannot see the log in your own.'" I added: "That was written around 50 A.D. Apparently, it takes time for these ideas to catch on."

The Dalai Lama is often one of the most reasonable voices we hear. When he spoke at a university here in New Jersey there were far more people trying to get tickets than there were seats to accommodate them. Most of those people have to have been at least nominally Christian. I wondered when they had been as eager to hear the teaching of Jesus.

Jesus, the Son of God, set the standard for a moral life; no other authority is necessary. If his teaching hasn't transformed the world, it isn't because another teacher is needed; it's because the world hasn't taken the Gospel to heart and put it into practice in everyday life. In the new beginning that Lent represents, we can commit ourselves to read the Gospel regularly, listen attentively as it is preached, profess it without shame when it is challenged or neglected, and proclaim it ourselves by how we live every moment of every day.

Live Lent!

I will prayerfully read the gospel passage to be proclaimed at next Sunday's Mass, and then I will listen attentively to the reading and the homily, all the while considering how the Scripture applies to my everyday life. I will talk to at least one other person about what insight I gained. I will sincerely try to make this a weekly practice. (Readings for daily Mass, including Sundays, can be found at www.usccb.org. Click on the date under "Daily Readings" on the right of the screen.

 Pray

Lord, Jesus Christ, you told Pontius Pilate that you came into the world to bear witness to the truth. Help me to always listen first to your teaching and to live according to your word, for you are truth itself. Amen.

Friday

 Pray

"Many are the troubles of the just man, but out of them all the LORD delivers him." (Psalm 34:20)

 Read *John 7:1-2, 10, 25-30*

Summary: *"So they tried to arrest him, but no one laid a hand upon him, because his hour had not yet come."* (John 7:30)

Spend two minutes in silence. Then repeat this passage from Scripture, and let it speak to your heart.

 Meditation

In the 1985 film *Witness*, an Amish family—as part of a chain of events following a murder in Philadelphia—shelters policeman John Book. While he is with the family, Book and three young Amish men are harassed by a group of toughs. The non-violent Amish take the harassment without responding, but John Book answers with his fists.

This scene raises a question: Are we to admire the Amish men who were humiliated or the cop who triumphed over the bullies? When we're watching a movie—so many of which involve violence responding to violence—the answer may seem clear. And, in fact, applause broke out in many theaters when that scene was shown.

But that is not the example Jesus gave us. In the gospel reading, we hear the rumblings of what will soon confront him: "Is he not the one they are trying to kill?" And we know that he will respond to betrayal, false accusations, verbal and physical abuse, and crucifixion with patience, and not with retaliation.

And what of us, who are unlikely to be in a spot like John Book's? When someone makes a caustic remark, do we feel compelled to answer with something a little sharper? When someone cuts us off on the road, do we feel compelled to speed up and get in front again? Do we applaud as the good guy annihilates the bad guys in so many of the films and digital games of our time? Or do we take the counsel of the apostle Peter: "Do not return evil for evil or reviling for reviling; but on the contrary bless, for to this you have been called" (1 Peter 3:9).

Live Lent!

I will resolve today not to patronize movies, television shows, electronic games, or any other media that present violence as admirable or heroic. I will pray for an end to violence in the world.

 Pray

Gentle Jesus, you taught us not to answer insult with insult or violence with violence, and you gave us a challenging example by not striking back at your enemies. May I apply your teaching and imitate your example in every aspect of my life. Amen.

Saturday

 Pray

"Let the malice of the wicked come to an end, but sustain the just, O searcher of heart and soul, O just God." (Psalm 7:10)

 Read *John 7:40-53*

Summary: *"So a division occurred in the crowd because of him. Some of them even wanted to arrest him, but no one laid hands on him. So the guards went to the chief priests and Pharisees, who asked them, 'Why did you not bring him?' The guards answered, 'Never before has anyone spoken like this man.'"* (John 7:43-46)

Spend two minutes in silence. Then repeat this passage from the Scripture, and let it speak to your heart.

Meditation

When Pope Francis made his first trip outside of Rome, in July 2013, he visited the island of Lampedusa off the southern coast of Italy. Lampedusa is a kind of way station for people fleeing poverty and conflict in North Africa. Thousands have drowned trying to cross the Mediterranean, and the pope said he felt compelled to visit to show his solidarity with the migrants, mourn those who had been lost, and pose a blunt question.

"Who is responsible for the blood of these brothers and sisters of ours?" he asked in a homily. "Nobody! That is our answer: It isn't me; I don't have anything to do with it; it must be someone else, but certainly not me. Yet God is asking each of us: 'Where is the blood of your brother which cries out to me?' Today no one in our world feels responsible; we have lost a sense of responsibility for our brothers and sisters."

Remarks like these on the part of Pope Francis call to mind what the guards told the Pharisees and chief priests concerning Jesus: "Never before has anyone spoken like this man!" It's an apt analogy, because the pope is simply repeating what Jesus himself taught us: "Love one another." Perhaps the world had gotten so used to that message—and so used to disregarding it—that it is shocked to hear it repeated in such challenging terms. The least that can be said is that the world is listening to Pope Francis. It remains to be seen whether the world will respond with indifference. But we need not wait to answer for ourselves, and there is no better time than Lent.

Live Lent!

I will seek a way as a volunteer or as a donor, or both, to directly serve the poor in my vicinity. I will include the poor in all of my prayers.

 Pray

You taught us that this is the whole law, to love God and to love all people as brothers and sisters. Help me to remember that to love as you love is to love without discrimination or condition. Help me to treat others needs as though they were my own. Amen.

Fifth Sunday of Lent

The passion foretold

Suggested Environment

A small table with a burning candle, a cross, and a Bible opened to the gospel reading for this session. Consider decorating the table with violet, the liturgical color of the Lenten Season.

Liturgical Readings for the Fifth Sunday of Lent

JEREMIAH 31:31-34
"I will remember their sin no more"

PSALM 51:3-4, 12-13, 14-15 (12A)
"Give me back the joy of your salvation"

HEBREWS 5:7-9
"He learned obedience through suffering"

JOHN 12:20-33
"I will draw everyone to myself"

Focus

Living well means letting go of self-interest so that others may life more fully.

Opening Song (To download, visit ocp.org/renew-music.)
"Create in Me," Bob Hurd, Anawim

Opening Prayer

Divide the group in two, and pray alternately from Psalm 51, with everyone repeating the response:

R. **Create a clean heart in me, O God.**

Side 1: *Have mercy on me, O God, in your goodness;*
in the greatness of your compassion wipe out my
offense.

Thoroughly wash me from my guilt
and of my sin cleanse me.

R. **Create a clean heart in me, O God.**

Side 2: *A clean heart create for me, O God,*
and a steadfast spirit renew within me.

Cast me not out from your presence,
and your Holy Spirit take not from me.

R. **Create a clean heart in me, O God.**

Side 1: *Give me back the joy of your salvation,*
and a willing spirit sustain in me.

I will teach transgressors your ways,
and sinners shall return to you.

R. **Create a clean heart in me, O God.**

The Gospel of the Lord

"Amen, amen, I say to you, unless a grain of wheat falls to the ground and dies, it remains just a grain of wheat." (John 12:24a)

Read *aloud John 12: 20-33*

Reflect

What word, phrase, or image from the scripture reading touches your heart or connects to your experience?

Share with the group, or write your response here:

_____

_____

_____

_____

Old Testament Connections

In his remarks to Philip and Andrew, Jesus makes clear for the first time what is involved in his "hour," which is about to begin. Referring to himself as the "Son of Man," meaning the triumphant one who sits at the right hand of God (Daniel 7:14), he tells them that the grain of wheat must "die" before it bears fruit. It is familiar imagery for those who come from the grain-rich farmland of the Galilee.

Such ideas from the Old Testament abound in this passage, all related to the theme of "salvation." The prophets spoke to the crises of their time, but for the followers of Jesus and for the evangelists, the utterances of those ancient prophets shed light on God's plan of salvation as it had unfolded in the life and ministry of Jesus. This is not an original tactic developed by Christians. It is used constantly in the Old Testament as the prophets interpret the events of their time in light of God's earlier actions regarding Moses—God's selection of Moses to communicate the divine will to the Hebrews, and God's protection of his chosen people.

The words of Isaiah ring in the ears of Jesus' disciples as being marvelously fulfilled in their time. Isaiah of Jerusalem told King Ahaz that the Lord would give the king a sign of protection from his enemies: "Look, the virgin shall conceive and bear a son, and they shall name him Emmanuel" (Isaiah 7:14). It was divinely appropriate to apply this to Jesus as Matthew's Gospel did (Matthew 1:22). Second

---

[1] Isaiah of Jerusalem mentioned certain kings who reigned in the late eighth and early seventh centuries BC, chapters 1-39 in the Book of Isaiah. A second author called Second Isaiah addressed the exiled people in Babylon later in history. His work is thought to be found in the Book of Isaiah chapters 40-55. Some scholars see a "Third" Isaiah at work in chapters 56 to the end. Together, they constitute what are called the "School of Isaiah."

Isaiah, a later follower of Isaiah1, offered hope for refugees who had been forced to leave their homes with their infants and children at the points of spears and swords to live in a land of foreign language and customs. Matthew's Gospel reports that Jesus too was taken to Egypt by his parents to protect him from violence at the whim of King Herod (Matthew 2:13-15).

When Jesus says he will be "lifted up from the earth" (John 12:32), his words prepare us for his passion and death. For the community of John, it is an image to be gazed upon as we would contemplate a crucifix. In this Gospel, it is not so much a sorrowful image as one of hope. Jesus is lifted up as if mid-way in his ascent into heaven, the realm of the Father. The ascension begins on the cross.

Reflect

People in every country of this world display Christ on the cross. The more they suffer, the more this image of Jesus "lifted up from the earth" seems to give meaning to their lives. How does the cross give meaning to the suffering you have endured?

Share with the group, or write your response here.

_____

_____

_____

_____

 Meditation

Four months after my brother Paul was diagnosed with metastasized bladder cancer, he was in the hospital suffering from pain. His "hour had come," and he knew it. He was the father of 7 and the grandfather of 13 and had lived a full life. However, we, his family, were in disbelief and shock at the suddenness of his deterioration. I think he was too. We did not want to believe he was dying. He had spent his life giving to his family and to his work as a teacher and coach.

Two days before he passed away, Paul rallied and asked to speak privately with his wife of more than 50 years and their eldest son. He spoke of his deep love for his wife and each of his children, and then he told his eldest, "Take care of your mother" and, most importantly, "do not fight with her." He then told my nephew, "Love your two boys, and bring them up with good moral values and faith." Paul asked his son to kiss him goodbye. My nephew believed he was a little boy the last time he had kissed his dad.

The origin of the word "good-bye" is the blessing "God be with you." My brother, a man of faith, assured his beloved wife and oldest child that all would be well—that God was with them. Paul had found the grace to finally let go of life, and he passed on his rich legacy of faith and service to his family, his friends, and his former students and players—the myriad people who came to his funeral services and testified to the impact he had made on their lives. Six of his former players were his pall bearers. They towered over the congregation as they carried their coach into the church for his funeral Mass. Paul was a simple guy who spent his life for others, and people remembered.

In today's gospel reading, Jesus declares that his "hour has come" and introduces the first set of teachings about the meaning of his death. This parable helps us understand Jesus' death by setting up a contrast between remaining solitary, "just a grain of wheat," and "bearing much fruit." In John's Gospel, "fruit" is Jesus' metaphor for the faith community. He proclaims, using the image of the seed, that only by spending life do we keep it. He insists that those who hoard their lives will lose them in the end, and those who spend their lives will gain them in the end. The grain of wheat is not fruitful if it is preserved, protected, and secure. It is when the grain is scattered in the cold ground, and buried there as if in a tomb, that it bears fruit. Two bushels of seed and an acre yields enough wheat for about 2,500 loaves of bread that would feed lots of hungry people. The result is remarkable not only because a dead seed generates life, but because it generates so much life. Jesus' death gave birth to the Church, the community of Jesus' disciples, and reveals the power and promise of God and God's love for the world.

Jesus in his last hour gave up everything as he hung on the cross for us and for the world. He spent his life for others. His death on the cross evoked his prayer at the Last Supper: "This is my body, given up for you." He might have thought that his mission was a failure, that his efforts to teach his disciples were insufficient, that his preaching hadn't taken hold. He might have given up his hopes on the cross. But the final word is not the suffering, but the resurrection. The death of the seed leads to the wonder of the blade of wheat. The crucifixion leads to the wonder of the resurrection.

In Mitch Albom's book *Tuesdays With Morrie*, the title character, a consummate professor, has been diagnosed with ALS, and he is dying. He decides to teach people how to die. Mitch, a student of his from sixteen years before, renews their friendship and records Morrie's wise words. Morrie connects our capacity to live life abundantly with our ability to let go. He says that most of the time we just start to experience this "letting go" when, once we encounter risk, pain, or fear, we pull back. Morrie tells his student, "Feel it fully, and then let it go." And he cautions that our unwillingness to enter an experience fully destines us to feel only the fear, and to feel it alone. In the end, when my brother was facing death, he didn't shirk from the experience but faced it squarely, and with the freedom that gave him, he blessed his wife and children and the generations to follow with a rich legacy.

Jesus calls on us to die so that we might live, to let go so that we might be fruitful. Morrie grasps the heart of that teaching: The freedom of letting go of possessions, preoccupations, conveniences, security— all so that others might live more fully—is not about dying well, but about living well.

Reflect

What does Jesus teach us in the parable of the seed about living? About dying?

_____

_____

_____

_____

Share a story of a deceased person who passed on to you a faith-filled legacy by living well.

_____

_____

_____

_____

What experience do you need to face squarely and then let go of so you can live more fully?

_____

_____

_____

_____

Live Lent!

Jesus did not hoard his life but gave it away freely. Commit to doing an act of kindness this Lent—giving away a bit of your time.

 Closing Prayer

Pray together:

God of promise and power, thank you for sending Jesus into the world to die for me and for all and for inviting me to be part of the community of disciples. I pray in gratitude for sharing the gift of Jesus' life, the gift that leads to eternal life. Give me the grace of letting go of possessions, preoccupations, conveniences, and security—all so that others might live more fully. Help me to live well and more fully by giving myself more completely to you. Amen.

Looking Ahead

To prepare for the next session, read the following:

- Palm Sunday of the Lord's Passion: A generous and loving gesture
- Mark 14:1-9

Monday

Pray

"Even though I walk in the dark valley I fear no evil; for you are at my side. . . ." (Psalm 23:4)

Read John 8:1-11

Summary: *"Jesus said, 'Nor do I condemn you. You may go. But from now on, avoid this sin."* (John 8:11b)

Spend two minutes in silence. Then repeat this passage from Scripture, and let it speak to your heart.

Meditation

In the never-ending tension between Peanuts characters Charlie Brown and Lucy Van Pelt, Lucy tells Charlie on one occasion, "I'm right, and you're wrong, and it's as simple as that!"

But even if Lucy was right in that case, it's seldom as simple as that. We see why in today's gospel story.

The bunch that brought the woman before Jesus said that she had been "caught in the very act" of adultery, and if that was true, then they were right: the Law of Moses prescribed that adulteresses be punished. It was as simple as that.

We can infer from Lucy's tone that she felt that her fix on the truth gave her some power over Charlie Brown, and that's often the unhealthy byproduct of being right and knowing it.

The accusers in the Gospel had an ulterior motive; they wanted to maneuver Jesus into contradicting the Law.

They didn't care about the woman and, theoretically at least, would have been more willing to see her die than see her acknowledge her mistake and try to reform.

But Jesus was not the prophet of "I'm right, and it's a simple as that."

Jesus was the prophet of mercy, patience, forgiveness, and repentance.

He reminded the men who had treated that woman so shabbily that she and they shared what we all share: human nature.

He reminded them that sharing human nature doesn't mean only sharing an inclination to disregard the law of God and the wellbeing of others; it also means the potential, with God's grace, to correct ourselves, and to live in hope rather than in despair.

That's why we observe Lent—not simply to admit that we have sinned, but to ask for God's inexhaustible mercy and move on to live as witnesses to his love.

Live Lent!

When I hear in the news about persons accused or convicted of serious crimes, I will entrust them to public authorities and to the mercy of God, and forgive them in my own heart.

 Pray

O God of justice, we are grateful for the generosity with which you accept our penitence and invite us to live as though reborn. May we always be worthy of your patience and forgiveness, and may we always extend our own forgiveness to others. Amen.

Tuesday

 Pray

"The nations shall revere your name, O Lord, and all the kings of the earth your glory." (Psalm 102:16)

 Read *John 8:21-30*

Summary: *"So Jesus said to them, 'When you lift up the Son of Man, then you will realize that I AM, and that I do*

---

nothing on my own, but I say only what the Father taught me.'" (John 8:28)

Spend two minutes in silence. Then repeat this passage from Scripture, and let it speak to your heart.

 Meditation

In his 1983 movie *Zelig*, Woody Allen plays a man who is known as the "human chameleon." The sobriquet refers to the fact that the man, Leonard Zelig, so pines for acceptance that he takes on the physical characteristics and demeanors of the people around him—kitchen servants, party animals of the "roaring '20s", Nazis of pre-war Germany. Allen tells the fictional story in the style of a documentary that portrays the attempts by a psychiatrist to raise Zelig's self-esteem so that he doesn't need to seek comfort in the identities of others.

Zelig portrays an absurdly extreme case of a real phenomenon that can occur with various degrees of severity—the lack of a strong sense of self, confusion about or discomfort with who a person is. In the passage from John's Gospel, however, we meet a person whose sense of self could not be more clear. Our faith tells us what John's Gospel expresses from its first verse: that Jesus is both God and man, that his ministry on earth is God's ministry on earth, that his words are God's words. Jesus emphasizes his certainty about that every time he uses the expression "I AM," which Catholic scholars tell us alludes to a Hebrew term for God.

Although some skeptics try to dilute the identity of Jesus by conceding only that he was a wise teacher or an insightful prophet, we know better. The Jesus we encounter in his word, in the Eucharist, and in the quiet times of our Lenten practice shares our human nature and unites it intimately, inseparably, with the nature of God. Jesus knows who he is, and we are his disciples because we know too.

Live Lent!

I will take time today to pray the Nicene Creed; I will pause after each phrase concerning the identity of Jesus, meditating on who he is, what he has done for me, and what I am called to do as his friend and disciple.

Pray

Almighty God, by coming in to the world in the person of Jesus, you have demonstrated the depths of your love for us and shown us the value you place on the human person. Help me to imitate in my own humanity the example of holiness and compassion set by Jesus. Amen.

Wednesday

 Pray

"Blessed are you, O Lord, the God of our fathers, praiseworthy and exalted above all forever; And blessed is your holy and glorious name, praiseworthy and exalted above all for all ages." (Daniel 3:52)

 Read *John 8:31-42*

Summary: *"I tell you what I have seen in the Father's presence; then do what you have heard from the Father." (John 8:38)*

Spend two minutes in silence. Then repeat this passage from Scripture, and let it speak to your heart.

Meditation

In the 1951 musical *The King and I*, a nineteenth-century king of Siam finds his equilibrium disrupted by an English tutor he has hired to educate his children. The teacher introduces ideas about personal freedom, gender equality, and scientific inquiry that are foreign to the closed society of Siam, and the king at first resists them. He expresses his discomfiture in lyrics written by Oscar Hammerstein II: "When I was a boy, world was better spot. What was so was so, what was not was not." But eventually the king, who wants his country to be respected among the community of nations, realizes that he cannot achieve his goal unless he is willing to open himself and his people to the pursuit of truth.

The self-assurance that had kept the king in an archaic mind set provides a metaphor for the converts who debated with Jesus in the episode described in John's Gospel. Those folks thought they were righteous just because they were "descendants of Abraham"—that they did not have to live up to the moral challenge Jesus was preaching. They wanted the security of being children of God without confronting the truth of what God expected of them.

In our own time, people can be misled by a similar self-assurance, so set on their autonomy that they see no need to measure their lives by the standard of the Gospel, the standard of submission to God's will and unselfish service to other human beings. May our Lenten observance recommit us to the generous, expansive life envisioned by the One who created us, and not to a far more limited life that we design for ourselves.

Live Lent!

I will meditate on Jesus' command "that you love one another" and experience the freedom of an unprovoked act of kindness or generosity.

 Pray

Lord Jesus Christ, you call us to escape the prison of self-absorption and live in the freedom of compassion and generosity. Help me to live the Gospel by imitating you, who showed us what it means to love one another. Amen.

Thursday

 Pray

"He remembers forever his covenant which he made binding for a thousand generations—which he entered into with Abraham. ..."
(Psalm 105:8-9a)

Read *John 8:51-59*

Summary: *"Jesus said to them, 'Amen, amen, I say to you, before Abraham came to be, I AM.' So they picked up stones to throw at him; but Jesus hid and went out of the temple area." (John 8:58-59)*

Spend two minutes in silence. Then repeat this passage from Scripture, and let it speak to your heart.

Meditation

Many years ago, a friend of mine, a rabbi, left his congregation to take up a hospital ministry in another state. I was one of twelve speakers at a farewell program at his synagogue. My family attended. The kids, who knew nothing of this or any other rabbi, sat quietly through the testimonials. But after the program had concluded, and the rabbi walked over to greet us, my pre-teen daughters—after hearing about his impact on individuals and a whole community—both rushed up to him and hugged him as though he were an uncle or grandfather.

That scene—Christian children embracing a Jewish elder—is a helpful image to keep in mind in these next few days when we hear so much in the Gospels about "the Jews" persecuting Jesus. The first reading at today's Mass (Genesis 17:3-9) is the account of God's covenant with Abraham, the father of the Jewish people, and his descendants, a covenant that God says—and the Catholic Church teaches—will last until the end of time. And as Jesus implies in the Gospel passage, the Jewish faith was the tree from which the Christian faith took root and flourished. And the fact that certain religious leaders were antagonistic toward Jesus and wanted to stifle him in no way impugns Judaism itself or all Jewish people then or now.

Gospel passages that we will read between now and Good Friday have been carelessly or deliberately misconstrued so as to justify unspeakable atrocities against Jews. As we contemplate the passion of Jesus, let us also contemplate the passion of the people from whom he was born to be the savior of the world.

Live Lent!

I will read Genesis 17:3-9 and pray for the safety and well-being of Jewish people everywhere.

 Pray

Almighty God, may hatred for the Jewish people be eradicated from the minds of human beings. No matter our faith, may our love for you and our love for each other be the only motivation for our actions. We ask this through Jesus Christ, our Lord. Amen.

Friday

 Pray

"I love you, O Lord, my strength, O Lord, my rock, my fortress, my deliverer." (Psalm 18:2-3A)

 **Read** *John 10:31-42*

Summary: *"If I do not perform my Father's works, do not believe me; but if I perform them, even if you do not believe me, believe the works, so that you may realize and understand that the Father is in me and I am in the Father." (John 10:37-38)*

Spend two minutes in silence. Then repeat this passage from Scripture, and let it speak to your heart.

 Meditation

A small gaggle of customers in my family's grocery store were killing part of a Saturday morning by gossiping about our pastor. According to the chatter, the priest was undignified, abrupt, cheap, obese, and obsessed with fundraising. When the merry party had dispersed, a man who worked for my family muttered to me, "When he's gone, they'll erect a statue of him and swear he was a saint."

It didn't work out exactly that way—there was no statue—but fifty years later I still hear people speak highly of him. He served the parish for 25 years, sleeping on an army cot in a small office when he first arrived. He built a rectory, a new church, and a convent, and he converted the old church into the town's first Catholic school. When I say "he built" I don't mean it figuratively. He swept and shoveled and swung a hammer, wielded a wrecking bar, and spread concrete. And this in spite of an advanced case of arthritis. He also celebrated liturgies with care and preached with energy, and he was accessible, good-natured, and friendly.

When Father died, our bishop said in the funeral homily that diocesan records showed that our pastor had less personal wealth when he retired than he did when he emerged from the seminary. Clearly, Father was interested in only one thing—doing God's works. He had his model in Jesus, who did God's works despite indifference, criticism, and threats to his life. We shouldn't let Lent slip away without asking ourselves how well we imitate that model—because it was meant for us, too.

Live Lent!

Before Easter Sunday, I will do something that clearly is the Father's work: directly aid the poor, bring gifts to a nursing home, visit an elderly person who lives alone, ask my pastor what task most badly needs doing in the parish—and either do it myself or arrange to get it done. I will write myself a short letter explaining how the prospect of doing this work will affect my experience of Holy Week.

 Pray

Lord Jesus, you asked your persecutors to judge you based on whether you did the works of the Father. May I be measured by the same standard, and may I be judged a faithful servant. Amen.

Pray

"He who scattered Israel, now gathers them together, he guards them as a shepherd his flock." (Jeremiah 31:10b)

 Read *John 11:45-56*

Summary: "(H)e prophesied that Jesus was going to die for the nation, and not only for the nation, but also to gather into one the dispersed children of God." (John 11:51b-52)

Spend two minutes in silence. Then repeat this passage from Scripture, and let it speak to your heart.

Meditation

The director of the diaconate in my diocese started a weekly free pasta dinner served largely by deacons. One of the regular dinner guests approached one evening, asked my name, and then asked, "What color do you most like to wear?" Black, I told her, and she said that she would crochet for me a black scarf and hat. I learned that she had been making hats and scarfs for all the deacons who serve that meal, asking first for the man's name and favorite color.

Hand-making those items for us was magnanimous, but the gesture was more meaningful because this woman made each hat and scarf for an individual person. Her generosity reminded me of a point made by Pope Francis when he was preaching on the Gospel passage we read today. The pope was reflecting on the gospel writer's interpretation of what Caiaphas told the Sanhedrin: " 'It is better for you that one man should die instead of the people, so that the whole nation may not perish.' He did not say this on his own," the Gospel continues, "but since he was high priest for that year, he prophesied that Jesus was going to die for the nation, and not only for the nation, but also to gather into one the dispersed children of God."

Pope Francis said that the evangelist's observation that Jesus died "for the dispersed children of God" means that Jesus died literally for each one of us, individually—by name, as it were. Jesus' act of love, which we will commemorate next week, was not generic; it was personal. He didn't die for an idea. He died for you. He died for me.

Live Lent!

I will take time today to pray the Stations of the Cross, reminding myself that each step Jesus took, he took for me. I will conclude by meditating on how I might return that love through personal acts of generosity and compassion. (There are audio and written Stations of the Cross available at http://www.usccb.org/prayer-and-worship/prayers-and-devotions/stations-of-the-cross/)

 Pray

Lord Jesus Christ, I worship you as my God, and I embrace you as my loving friend. May my life be a reflection of the warmth with which you care for me and for each of your brothers and sisters. Amen.

A generous and loving gesture

Suggested Environment

A small table with a burning candle and a Bible opened to the gospel reading for this session. Consider decorating the table with red, the liturgical color of Passion Sunday, or violet, the liturgical color of the Lenten season.

Liturgical Readings for
Palm Sunday of the Passion of the Lord

ISAIAH 50:4-7
"The Lord God helps me"

PSALM 22:8-9, 17-18, 19-20, 23-24
"They have pierced my hands and my feet"

PHILIPPIANS 2:6-11
"He humbled himself to the point of death"

MARK 14:1-15:47
"She has anticipated my burial"

Focus

God loves us with an extravagant love.

Opening Song (To download, visit ocp.org/renew-music.)
"Behold the Wood," Dan Schutte

✠ Opening Prayer

Divide the group in two, and pray together from Psalm 22, with everyone repeating the response:

R. **My God, my God, why have you abandoned me?**

Side 1: All who see me scoff at me;
they mock me with parted lips,
they wag their heads:

"He relied on the LORD; let him deliver him,
let him rescue him, if he loves him."

R. **My God, my God, why have you abandoned me?**

Side 2: Many dogs surround me,
a pack of evildoers closes in upon me;

They have pierced my hands and my feet;
I can count all my bones.

R. **My God, my God, why have you abandoned me?**

Side 1: They divide my garments among them,
and for my vesture they cast lots.

But you, O LORD, be not far from me;
O my help, hasten to aid me.

R. **My God, my God, why have you abandoned me?**

Side 2: I will proclaim your name to my brethren;
in the midst of the assembly I will praise you:

"You who fear the LORD, praise him;
all you descendants of Jacob, give glory to him;
revere him, all you descendants of Israel!"

R. **My God, my God, why have you abandoned me?**

📖 The Gospel of the Lord

"The poor you will always have with you, and whenever you wish you can do good to them, but you will not always have me." (Mark 14:7)

Read *aloud Mark 14:1-9*

Reflect

What word, phrase, or image from the scripture reading touches your heart or connects to your experience?

Share with the group, or write your response here:

_____

_____

_____

_____

Old Testament Connections

The ancient Hebrews practiced anointing with oil as a sign that a person had been called to an elevated position—specifically, a priest, a prophet, or a king. The Book of Exodus (30:22-25) contains a formula for how the anointing oil was to be made. Someone anointed with oil made in keeping with this instruction was thought to have received "the Spirit of the Lord."

In perhaps the most familiar example in the Old Testament, the prophet Samuel anointed first Saul and then David as king of Israel (1 Samuel). A priest or a king who had been marked in this way was sometimes called "the anointed one," the "Mashiah"—a term that took on a special meaning as Israel awaited a savior sent by God. Jewish religious law forbade anointing of an "ordinary" person, someone who was neither priest nor king (Exodus 30:33). This restriction no doubt helped stoke the passions of the critics who berated the woman who anointed Jesus, in the episode Mark describes.

Jesus, already anticipating his death, saw this anointing as preparation of his body for burial. Perhaps this woman, well aware of the antagonism directed at Jesus, saw it the same way. "She knew that were she to follow her heart in drawing near to him she would not be rejected," writes Father David Reid in a forthcoming book on the Gospel of Mark, part of the RENEW Scripture Series. " His vigorous defense of her flooded her soul with every word of every Psalm she had prayed. If ever there was an innocent man who did God's will, he was Jesus. She cast her lot with him. Israel's psalms, Israel's lamentation, is precisely the experience of being caught in someone's evil plotting. She was not focused on the enemy, but on the one who would die. She wanted God to raise him up. She would do her part—anoint him."

Reflect

Jesus is still crucified today in the sense that so many ignore, reject, or ridicule his teaching. Why and how do you emulate the woman from Bethany by casting your lot with Jesus amid the indifference and scorn? *Share with the group, or write your response here.*

_____

_____

_____

_____

 Meditation

By the 1990's the HIV/AIDS epidemic had seen millions of people infected (many of them unknowingly) around the globe. Those who contracted AIDS had to live not only with the devastating course of the disease but also with the attached social stigma. Many AIDS victims suffered from judgement and social isolation. At that time people were terrified that they would contract the disease through touch or air.

It was the early 90's, and I went to the hospital to visit a young man who had AIDS. I didn't know what to expect. I remember that as I haltingly entered his room, I was moved, as I witnessed his mom massaging her dying son's thin and frail body with oil. The young man died a few days later.

I knew the back story. The son had felt rejected by his family because he was gay, and he had moved away. When he became sick, he got in touch with his parents and asked if he could come home; he wanted, he said, to die with his family around him. The family welcomed him home. His mother reentered his life and lavished her love upon her dying son. She told me the gift of massaging her son not only gave him some relief but was healing for her—forgiveness and healing flowed from one to the other.

There is a parallel between this family's experience and that of the unnamed woman in the episode recounted by Mark. The woman from Bethany breaks the neck of her flask, and pours expensive oil on Jesus' head. The description of the oil as "costly" and "genuine" nard highlights the generosity and enthusiasm of the woman. It was the custom at that time to pour a few drops of perfumed oil on a guest's head when he arrived at a house or sat down for a meal. This woman did not just sprinkle a bit of oil on Jesus but broke her jar and anointed him with the full contents. In the other gospel accounts of this incident, she also pours oil on Jesus' feet and then washes his feet with her hair. She lavishes her unbridled love upon Jesus. Love and mercy flow between them.

Some of the guests were angry by her extravagant action. They thought the woman was wasteful and that the money could have been used for the poor. I am sure there were also some who were moved by her loving service to Jesus and that some may have just tolerated it but wondered why she needed to put more than a few drops of oil on his head. I also think others might have been wondering how this unknown woman managed to get into the party, much less close to Jesus. Whatever their reasons, they scolded her, but Jesus came to her defense. He knew her heart and experienced her impulsive act of love as a gift and her kindness as a healing balm. How he must have needed that love as he prepared for his passion and death.

Ironically, although Jesus raises up this woman as one whose deed will be remembered wherever the Gospel is proclaimed, most Christians are more familiar with Judas than with this faithful disciple. The account of Judas's betrayal immediately follows this section of the passion. Her story is found only in Mark's version of the Passion which is read every three years on Palm Sunday during Cycle B. Often, pastors choose the shorter form of the Passion, thus eliminating her story.

The world would be a more compassionate place if there were more people like this anonymous woman who acted on the impulse of love. She would not stop the flow of love because of what people thought of her. Many times, we think of doing something kind for someone and then do not act. It may be because we are bashful or feel awkward about it. We may second guess ourselves or just get busy and put a thoughtful action aside. It may be the simplest of actions—the impulse to send a thank-you card, the impulse to tell someone of our love or gratitude, the impulse to visit a person who is homebound or sick in the hospital. It may be the impulse to love and accept someone we have judged as outside the bounds of our love. If love is true, there must always be a certain extravagance to it.

Lent is a time to reflect on how we can be more reckless in our loving—loving God, our neighbor, and ourselves.

Reflect

What touched you in the story about the mother and her son who had AIDS?

_____

_____

_____

_____

Explore why the guests were angry at the woman. What was Jesus' response to their judgement of the woman?

_____

_____

_____

_____

Name a person who is extravagant in showing his or her love but does it silently or anonymously.

_____

_____

_____

_____

Share a time you had an impulse to do a loving action, and you did it.

_____

_____

_____

_____

Live Lent!

✝ If you have in impulse to do a loving action this week, do it!

✝ Is there a person in your family whom you have cut off? Reach out to that person this week.

✝ Attend one or more of the Holy Week services—Holy Thursday, Good Friday, the Easter Vigil.

Closing Prayer

Pray together:

Loving God, you are extravagant in your love for us. Help me to experience your love in a deeper way as we enter Holy Week and reflect on your passion, death, and resurrection. I thank you for your willingness to love us unto death, death on a cross. Give me the grace to act on impulses to love with generosity and exuberance. Amen.

Monday

 Pray

"The Lord is my light and my salvation; whom should I fear? The Lord is my life's refuge; of whom should I be afraid?" (Psalm 27:1)

 Read *John 12:1-11*

Summary: *"You always have the poor with you, but you do not always have me."* (John 12:8)

Spend two minutes in silence. Then repeat this passage from Scripture, and let it speak to your heart.

Meditation

In 2005, ten bottles of Clive Christian No. 1 perfume were offered for sale in one store in London and another in New York. One 16.9-ounce bottle, adorned with diamonds and 18-carat gold, was priced at $205,000—but that included delivery. The value of perfume is ultimately determined by what someone is willing to pay for it.

Judas implied that the perfumed oil Mary used to anoint Jesus was worth three hundred days' wages. He might have been exaggerating, but the Gospel describes the oil as "costly," and that is all we need to know. It tells us that Mary was willing to pay a high price because of the value she placed on Jesus, who had taught her the Good News and raised her brother, Lazarus, to new life.

When Judas complained that the oil should have been sold to raise money for the poor, Jesus gave a paradoxical answer: "You always have the poor with you, but you do not always have me." It sounded as if Jesus were making himself more important than the poor, contradicting his own teaching. But this remark was addressed to Judas, and the writer, in a bitter comment that is almost unique in the Gospels, tells us that Judas didn't care about the poor; he cared only about enriching himself and was willing to sell even Jesus himself.

In Matthew's Gospel, Jesus tells us, "Where your treasure is, there also will your heart be." If we—like Mary and unlike poor Judas—value the presence of Jesus in our lives and put his teaching into practice, then we will also value the poor and do everything we can to help them.

Live Lent!

I will write a letter to myself, honestly listing the things in life that are of greatest value to me and the things in life that occupy most of my time, energy, and material resources. I will pray about whether I am satisfied with these lists and, if not, what I can do to re-order them.

 Pray

Almighty God, you have given us existence itself, life, an immortal soul, and the ministry and sacrifice of your son, Jesus Christ. Help me to value these gifts above all things and to show my gratitude by being a gift to others in my everyday life. Amen.

Tuesday

 Pray

"In you, O LORD, I take refuge; let me never be put to shame. In your justice rescue me, and deliver me; incline your ear to me, and save me." (Psalm 71:1-2)

 Read *John 13:21-33, 36-38*

Summary: *"After Judas took the morsel, Satan entered him. So Jesus said to him, 'What you are going to do, do quickly.' ... So Judas took the morsel and left at once. And it was night."* (John 13:27,30)

Spend two minutes in silence. Then repeat this passage from Scripture, and let it speak to your heart.

 **Meditation**

The 1936 movie *Prisoner of Shark Island* tells the story of Dr. Samuel Mudd, who was convicted of conspiracy in the murder of Abraham Lincoln. In this film, which portrays Mudd as innocent, a guard at the island fortress where Mudd is incarcerated, calls the doctor "Judas." The guard doesn't have to explain himself. Anyone who hears that name knows what it implies.

Judas Iscariot is the poster boy for betrayal—he betrayed the savior of the world, after all—and Christian society subjects him to a level of revulsion that it applies to few people. We noted in yesterday's reflection that even the evangelist felt at liberty to heap scorn on this man.

This unenviable status that Judas has achieved raises a question: Has he sunk so low that God would not forgive him? The answer may seem obvious, considering what Judas did, but in fact it is beyond our competence as it would be with respect to anyone else. We don't know anything about the interior life of Judas. We can't reconstruct his past, we can't know what was going on in his mind, and we can't know that he is beyond the reach of God's mercy. In fact, we can commend him to God's mercy, since we do not know for certain the judgment that God has passed on his life.

Pope Francis has stressed throughout his papacy that God's mercy is inexhaustible and that ours should be as well. If we want mercy for ourselves, we can ask it even for someone like Judas.

Live Lent!

I will identify two or three people—in history or in the world today—whose behavior has been in its own way almost as reprehensible as that of Judas. I will ask myself not if I can excuse their actions, but if I can forgive them and leave judgment in the hands of God. If I can do that, I will ask myself whom in my own life it is time to forgive. I will pray for God's mercy on all of us who have sinned and ask him to lift from my heart the weight of my judgment of others.

Pray

Merciful God, you alone can read the human heart; you alone know what moves us to act as we do. Thank you for your eagerness to forgive even the greatest of sinners. Give me the grace to bring my own sorrow and regrets to you, to sincerely repent my sins, and gratefully accept your forgiveness. Amen.

Wednesday

 Pray

"See, the Lord GOD is my help; who will prove me wrong?" (Isaiah 50:9a)

 Read *Matthew 26:14-25*

Summary: "When it was evening, he reclined at table with the Twelve. And while they were eating, he said, 'Amen, I say to you, one of you will betray me.' Deeply distressed at this, they began to say to him one after another, 'Surely it is not I, Lord?'" (Matthew 26:20-22)

Spend two minutes in silence. Then repeat this passage from Scripture, and let it speak to your heart.

 Meditation

Most of us probably know at least two Latin phrases: "E pluribus unum" and "Et tu, Brute?" The first appears on the Great Seal of the United States, and it is taken to mean both that one nation emerges from many states and that one nation emerges from a wide variety of people. The second one was made famous by William Shakespeare in his play *Julius Caesar*. It is uttered by Caesar when he sees among his assassins Marcus Junius Brutus, whom he had thought was his friend: "And you, Brutus?" Shakespeare wasn't the first Elizabethan to use this phrase, but ancient historians reported that Caesar said nothing when he was set upon by men bound to prevent him from becoming ruler of Rome for life.

Although the remark is fictional, it expresses a plaintive sentiment, the dismay after being betrayed by someone close. Jesus, in his human nature, no doubt experienced that feeling when Judas turned against him after having heard the good news. And although we don't fully understand the glorified Christ, we might imagine that he feels that twinge of pain whenever any one of us, having heard the Gospel, fails to carry it out in our lives.

Tomorrow we begin our commemoration of the events in which Christ sealed his covenant with us by giving himself to us, first in the Eucharist and then on the cross. It was a lot to give, but, he loved us—his friends— that much. We don't always return that love. Perhaps it would help us as we make the many decisions that direct our daily lives to keep before us the image of Jesus asking, "And you ….?"

Live Lent!

I will read one of the Gospel accounts of the crucifixion and death of Jesus, meditate on the depth of his love for me, and pray a fervent act of contrition.

 Pray

Lord Jesus, you gave your life for me and for all so that we might live together with God in eternity. If my friendship for you is imperfect, if I betray you at times, accept my contrition and my determination to always return to your side when I have wandered. Amen.

Holy Thursday

 Pray

"He loved his own in the world, and he loved them to the end." (John 13:1b)

Read *John 13:1-15*

Summary: "So when he had washed their feet and put his garments back on and reclined at table again, he said to them, 'Do you realize what I have done for you? You call me 'teacher' and 'master,' and rightly so, for indeed I am. If I, therefore, the master and teacher, have washed your feet, you ought to wash one another's feet. I have given you a model to follow, so that as I have done for you, you should also do.'"
(John 13:12-15)

Spend two minutes in silence. Then repeat this passage from Scripture, and let it speak to your heart.

Meditation

On my dresser is a coin bank, a miniature building, that belonged to my father. In the coin bank are about two dozen dimes that have been handled so much that the images on them are almost worn away. Dad kept this bank with its "thin dimes" on his own dresser, and it is for me an important memento of him.

We cherish such things to remember our loved ones by, and on this day we celebrate the remembrance par excellence—the Eucharist. The passage from St. Paul's letter to the Corinthians that is read in the liturgy this evening is the oldest account of the Last Supper—dating to at least 54 AD. The words, recorded close to the event itself, are repeated at every Mass. And everyone who comes to that Eucharistic meal is called not only to remember Jesus but to imitate him, to imitate the example of unselfish service he performed when he washed the feet of his apostles.

Jesus asked us to remember and to be him in the lives of those who need us.

Live Lent!

I will take time to consider how I can follow the example Jesus set on this night, and, if possible, I will attend the Mass of the Lord's Supper.

 Pray

Lord Jesus, you have given us the greatest remembrance of all—the gift of yourself in the Eucharist. May I always give thanks for that gift by living as you lived, a life of compassion and service. Amen.

Good Friday

 Pray

"Into your hands I commend my spirit; you will redeem me, O LORD, O faithful God." (Psalm 31:6)

 Read *John 18:1–19:42*

Summary: "After this, aware that everything was now finished, in order that the Scripture might be fulfilled, Jesus said, 'I thirst.' There was a vessel filled with common wine. So they put a sponge soaked in wine on a sprig of hyssop and put it up to his mouth. When Jesus had taken the wine, he said, 'It is finished.' And bowing his head, he handed over the spirit." (John 19:28-30)

Spend two minutes in silence. Then repeat this passage from Scripture, and let it speak to your heart.

Meditation

Sam M. Lewis was a prolific songwriter. Many of his lyrics have been forgotten; others are standards, including "For All We Know" and "I'm Sitting on Top of the World."

Lewis's most poignant song was "I Heard a Forest Praying." Lewis wrote that trees provide a play area for children, conceal a lovers' lane, and "shelter the tired and the weary." But then the lyric notes that men also have turned fields and forests into battlefields, and "Men took a tree—an innocent tree—and made a cross for him."

Lewis didn't have to mention Jesus' name. We know that the cross that arrests our attention today was the "tree" on which Jesus died. We need to recall that his death was the consequence of sin and that sin continues to cause him pain. But we also need to recall that, whatever were the motives of the men who made that cross, the only motive Jesus had for submitting to it was his inexhaustible love for us. He died in order to rise. He died so that we might rise with him. That's why, on this good Friday, we kiss the cross.

Live Lent!

As this holy time draws to a close, I will meditate on the sacrifice that Jesus made for me and think about the smaller deaths that I might die for others—others who seldom have a visitor or a phone call; those who are never made to feel needed or appreciated; those who might like to receive the Eucharist at home; those who might like a ride to church on Sunday. Maybe this Sunday. And I will try to attend the Liturgy of the Lord's Passion today.

 Pray

Lord Jesus, I recall with deep regret the pain you suffered out of love for us. May the image of your cross keep me from ever hurting you, and may it inspire me to give unselfishly of myself and be a source of new life to others. Amen.

Holy Saturday

 Pray

We were indeed buried with him through baptism into death, so that, just as Christ was raised from the dead by the glory of the Father, we too might live in newness of life. (Romans 6:4)

Read Mark 16:1-7

Summary: "When the sabbath was over,

> Mary Magdalene, Mary, the mother of James, and Salome bought spices so that they might go and anoint him. ...
>
> On entering the tomb they saw a young man sitting on the right side, clothed in a white robe, and they were utterly amazed.
>
> He said to them, 'Do not be amazed!
>
> You seek Jesus of Nazareth, the crucified. He has been raised; he is not here. Behold the place where they laid him.
>
> But go and tell his disciples and Peter, He is going before you to Galilee; there you will see him, as he told you.'"
>
> (Mark 16:1,5-7)

Spend two minutes in silence. Then repeat this passage from Scripture, and let it speak to your heart.

Meditation

"Something strange is happening—there is a great silence on earth today, a great silence and stillness. The whole earth keeps silence because the King is asleep. The earth trembled and is still because God has fallen asleep in the flesh and he has raised up all who have slept ever since the world began."

That is from an ancient homily that is included in the Office of Readings in The Liturgy of the Hours for this day. It refers to the Church's teaching that after his death Jesus visited the souls denied access to heaven since the sin of Adam, assuring them that redemption was at hand. During this time, according to the homily, the world waited breathlessly for what was to follow—resurrection!

The world on this Saturday probably is not still at all. Much of the world on this Saturday probably is not anticipating the resurrection but is busy with something else. But we can create that stillness for ourselves, taking the time to absorb the enormity of what God has done for us and what he has promised to do—restore us to new life no matter how often we may die in sin.

Live Lent!

I will share the reason for my joy today—He is risen, so that we may rise with him!

 Pray

Almighty God, you so loved the world that you gave up your only son to death so that we might share with you eternal life. May I always see my own desires and concerns in the light of this sacrifice. Amen.

Pray

"The right hand of the Lord is exalted; the right hand of the Lord has struck with power. I shall not die, but live, and declare the works of the Lord." (Psalm 118:16-17)

Read *John 20: 1-9*

Summary: *"Then the other disciple also went in, the one who had arrived at the tomb first, and he saw and believed."* (John 20:8)

Celebrate!

Share this table prayer with those you will eat with today.
Pray together:

> Christ has risen! Alleluia!
> Loving God, you who create all things
> and generously give us all we need,
> we praise you and thank you for being present with us now
> as we celebrate the resurrection of Jesus Christ, your Son.
>
> Thank you for accompanying us on our Lenten journey;
> please be with us during this Easter season, and always,
> as we strive to live as disciples of your Son.
>
> May the breaking of bread, today and every day,
> remind us of the Bread of Life, Jesus Christ,
> who died to atone for our sins
> and rose again so that we, too, may rise
> and live in your presence forever.
>
> O God, bless this food and we who share it,
> and be with those who cannot share it with us.

We ask this in the name of the same Jesus Christ,
who lives and reigns with you and the Holy Spirit,
one God, forever and ever. Amen.

Alleluia! Christ has risen!

APPENDIX

There are two solemnities and one feast that can fall during Lent. When they fall on Lenten weekdays, they are celebrated in place of the liturgy for those days. Meditations for these three days are included in this appendix. Check the liturgical calendar; in some jurisdictions, the dates on which these celebrations are held may be changed.

Feast of the Chair of St. Peter

FEBRUARY 22

 Pray

"Even though I walk in the dark valley I fear no evil; for you are at my side with your rod and your staff that give me courage." (Psalm 23:4)

 Read *Matthew 16:13-19*

Summary: *"'Who do people say that the Son of Man is?'*
They replied, 'Some say John the Baptist, others Elijah,
still others Jeremiah or one of the prophets.'
He said to them, 'But who do you say that I am?'
Simon Peter said in reply,
'You are the Christ, the Son of the living God.'"
(Matthew 16:13b-16))

Spend two minutes in silence. Then repeat this passage from Scripture, and let it speak to your heart.

 Meditation

Visiting the Basilica of St. Peter in Rome, especially for the first time, can be overwhelming. The sheer size of the structure—one of the largest churches in the world—the vaulted ceilings, the soaring dome, and the multitude of altars and heroic monuments can be difficult to absorb. Soaring in the apse of the church is the extraordinary monument designed by Gian Lorenzo Bernini and completed in 1666. The centerpiece of this altar is a gilt bronze reliquary in the shape of a chair; within is an actual wooden chair, traditionally venerated as the chair used by Peter, the chief of the apostles and the first bishop of Rome. This chair consists of several parts, including some that may date to the ninth century.

The Church has set aside this day—even when it falls during Lent—in order to reflect on that chair, not as an important object in itself but as a symbol of the unity that Jesus wanted for his followers. That unity is grounded in our shared faith in Jesus as the Son of God and the savior of the world, in our mutual commitment to live in keeping with his Gospel of love, and our identification with each other as members of his body, the Church. Whenever we sin, either by an overt act or by neglect, we harm the Body of Christ and undermine the unity Jesus prayed for. By contrast, as we refresh our relationship with God during Lent, we contribute new vitality to the life of the whole Church.

Live Lent!

Today, I will pray the Nicene Creed, reflecting after each phrase how my faith in the teachings of the Church unite me with Catholic men and women around the world and across time.

 Pray

Lord Jesus Christ, you prayed that your followers might be one as you and the Father are one. May I be an instrument of the unity you desire by remaining faithful to your Gospel and by witnessing to it through a life of service to others. Amen.

Solemnity of St. Joseph, Husband of Mary

MARCH 19

 Pray

"The promises of the LORD I will sing forever; through all

generations my mouth shall proclaim your faithfulness, For you have said, 'My kindness is established forever'; in heaven you have confirmed your faithfulness." (Psalm 89:2-3)

 **Read** *Matthew 1:16; 18-21; 24a*

Summary: *"When Joseph awoke, he did as the angel of the Lord had commanded him and took his wife into his home." (Matthew 1:24)*

Spend two minutes in silence. Then repeat this passage from Scripture, and let it speak to your heart.

Meditation

One characteristic of the Scriptures that frustrates many readers is that the authors provide so few details about most of the personalities they write about. In the Gospels, for instance, many would like to know more about the magi, Simeon and Anna, the individual apostles, Lazarus, or the wife of Pontius Pilate. And certainly many would like to know more about Joseph, the husband of Mary.

The solemnity we celebrate today, even during Lent, indicates the esteem in which the Church holds Joseph. But the Gospel of Mark doesn't mention him at all and the Gospel of John mentions him only in passing. We never hear him speak. All we know about him is contained in relatively few passages in the Gospels of Matthew and Luke, and we know nothing of him from the time Jesus was 12 years old.

But the evangelists were not writing biography in the modern sense of the word; they were writing the story of our salvation. They told us about Joseph only what they thought we needed to know. What we need to know is that Joseph was a devout man who observed the Law of God; that he was a just man whose only goal was to shield Mary from opprobrium when he learned that she was pregnant; that he was a faithful man who submitted to what he understood to be God's will; and that he was a courageous and responsible man who took care of his family under the most difficult circumstances.

We know enough to see Joseph as our model and to do our best to imitate his qualities, keeping faith with God as we navigate the twists and turns in our own lives. .

Live Lent!

I will spend time reflecting on decisions I make in everyday life and major decisions I may have to make in the foreseeable future. I will ask the Holy Spirit to help me understand God's will before I make any significant choice.

 Pray

Almighty God, you chose Joseph as the guardian of Jesus and his mother, Mary. Help me, like Joseph, to always see clearly the role you have chosen for me and to carry it out according to your will. Amen.

Solemnity of the Annunciation of the Lord

MARCH 25

 Pray

"To do your will, O my God, is my delight, and your law is within my heart." (Psalm 40:9)

 Read Luke 1:26-38

Summary: *"You shall conceive and bear a son and give him the name Jesus. Great will be his dignity and he will be called the Son of the Most High."* (Luke 1:31-32)

Spend two minutes in silence. Then repeat this passage from Scripture, and let it speak to your heart.

 Meditation

I grew up in the 1940s and 1950s when everyday conversation wasn't nearly as candid as it is now.

For example, many people wouldn't say the word "pregnant," using a euphemism such as "expecting" instead.

When Lucille Ball became pregnant with her second child in 1952, the pregnancy was written into the story line of "I Love Lucy," but CBS wouldn't let the actors use the word "pregnant."

Well, when we celebrate the solemnity that interrupts the sober mood of Lent today, we don't pull any punches. This celebration is about the fact that Mary was pregnant. The Church makes that clear by placing this observance on March 25—nine months before Christmas.

Mary was pregnant, and she was going to experience the growth of the child within her and give birth to him—a human being who came into the world as a human being does.

Jesus, the son she conceived and carried and gave birth to, would experience everything it is to be a human being—except sin.

He would grow. He would study and learn. He would work. He would embark on a ministry that thrilled and comforted some and irritated and alienated others.

He would suffer, and he would die, and he would disappear from view—as every human being does.

It was no illusion. Jesus, Mary's son, was a human being. But he was also the Divine Being, the Second Person of the Trinity, God—and death could not contain him, as we will celebrate in two weeks, and because of his sacrifice and triumph, neither can death contain us.

Live Lent!

I will pray in thanksgiving that God really took on human form and became one of us, so that we might be freed from the power of sin and death and live in his company forever.

 Pray

Almighty God, you came into the world in human form to overcome for us the consequences of sin and death. May we live in a way that shows our gratitude for your Son's sacrifice on our behalf, and may we die with confidence in the power of the resurrection. Amen.

ABOUT THE AUTHORS

Sr. Theresa Rickard, OP, President and Executive Director of RENEW International, is a Dominican Sister of Blauvelt, New York. She holds the degree of Doctor of Ministry in Preaching from Aquinas Institute of Theology in St. Louis, Missouri. Additionally, she earned the degree of Master of Divinity from Union Theological Seminary in New York City and the degree of Master of Arts in Religion and Religious Education from Fordham University, New York City.

Sr. Terry is a national speaker, preacher, and author. She has written two Advent and Lent devotionals in the *Living Gospel* series published by Ave Maria Press. She is also a contributing author to *Preaching in the Sunday Assembly* and *We Preach Christ Crucified*, published by Liturgical Press. Sr. Terry is a regular contributor to the RENEW International blog under the title "God in the Stuff of Life," and you can follower her on Twitter at @SrTerryRickard.

Before joining the RENEW staff, she ministered in two parishes in the South Bronx and was the Director of Vocation and Formation Ministry for her Dominican congregation. She also was a member of the Archdiocese of New York Parish Mission Team.

Charles Paolino, a graduate of Seton Hall University and the Pennsylvania State University, is managing editor at RENEW International and a permanent deacon of the Diocese of Metuchen. He has written two Lenten devotionals in the *Living Gospel* series published by Ave Maria Press and is a columnist for *The Catholic Spirit*, the newspaper of the Diocese of Metuchen.

Presenting RENEW International

The RENEW process, both parish-based and diocese-wide, was developed and implemented in the Archdiocese of Newark, New Jersey. Its success there led other dioceses to bring RENEW to their people in over 160 dioceses in the United States and 24 countries throughout the world.

RENEW International has grown organically from its original single RENEW process. Materials and training have been inculturated and made available in more than 40 languages. We have added specific pastoral outreach to campuses and to young adults in their 20s and 30s. We have incorporated prison ministry and provided resources for the visually impaired.

The very core of all these processes remains the same: to help people become better hearers and doers of the Word of God. We do this by encouraging and supporting the formation of small communities that gather prayerfully to reflect on and share the Word of God, to make better connections between faith and life, and to live their faith more concretely in family, work, and community life.

As a not-for-profit organization, we sustain our pastoral outreach in part from the sales of our publications and resources and stipends for services we provide to parishes and dioceses. However, our priority is always to serve all parishes that desire to renew their faith and build the Church, regardless of their economic situation. We have been able to fulfill this mission not only in the inner- city and rural areas of the United States, but also in the developing world, especially Latin America and Africa, thanks to donations and charitable funding.

As you meet in your small group, we invite you to take a few moments to imagine the great invisible network of others, here in the United States and on other continents. They gather, as you do, in small Christian communities, around the Word of God present in the Scripture, striving to hear and act upon that Word. Keep them in your prayer: a prayer of thanksgiving for the many graces we have experienced; a prayer that the Holy Spirit will guide all of us as we Live Lent!

The Structure and Flow of a Session

A faith-sharing session typically lasts about 90 minutes. The following outline for your weekly small-group meeting suggests how your time might be allocated in order to keep the group moving smoothly from one element to the next. The time frame described here is based on the assumption that participants have read the session beforehand and considered their responses to the sharing questions, making notes in the spaces provided. Of course, the group leader may adjust the timing according to the dynamics of a particular session.

More detailed suggestions for the leader are included in *Essentials for Small Group Leaders* and *Leading Prayer in Small Groups,* both available from RENEW International. For details, visit www.renewintl.org.

Introductions · 5 minutes

If the group has not met before, if participants do not know each other, or if someone new has joined, an opportunity to get acquainted is important. People share most easily when they feel comfortable and accepted in a group.

Focus · 5 minutes

Read the focus to call to mind the central theme of the session.

Opening Song · 5 minutes

Play a song recommended for the session or a song of your own choosing.

Opening Prayer · 5 minutes

A few moments of silence should precede the prayer, which is always at the heart of gatherings of Christians.

Gospel Reading and Reflection · 20 minutes

A member of the group proclaims the Gospel. After a few minutes of silent reflection, the leader asks if anyone would like to share on the passage.

Old Testament Connection and Reflection • 20 minutes

Members of the group take a few minutes to review the Old Testament Connection, or a member of the group may read it aloud; then those who wish share their responses to the question. This section is not a discussion of the Old Testament reading for the day's Mass, but rather a reflection on the background in Hebrew Scriptures for the Gospel reading of the day.

Meditation • 25 minutes

Members of the group take a few minutes to review the Meditation, or a member of the group may read it aloud. Members review or consider their answers to the questions; then they share their responses to one or more of the questions.

Closing Prayer • 5 minutes

Note on the music

Songs are suggested for the moments of prayer at the opening of each small-group Sunday session. Music selections for *Live Lent!* are provided by our partners at OCP. The music is available as individual songs or as a nine-song digital album or "virtual CD." The individual songs and the digital album are available for purchase through RENEW International at ocp.org/renew-music.

from RENEW International

Live Lent! Year A, B, C

Continue your Lenten journey with the other titles in this series for lectionary years B and C.

All three titles are written by RENEW's own Sister Terry Rickard. *Live Lent!* will help you make the most of this season of preparation and spiritual renewal.

- Gather weekly in small groups
- Get inspired by the Sunday Gospel readings
- Explore Old Testament insights
- Reflect and pray **each day of the week**
- Take action in everyday life

Advent Awakenings

Advent is a time of spiritual anticipation amidst the often distracting preparations for Christmas. Stay focused on the significance of this season with *Advent Awakenings*, a four-session faith-sharing experience grounded in the Sunday gospel readings.

The *Advent Awakening* series is based on the three-year cycle of the Lectionary. Each book contains four sessions corresponding with the four Sundays of Advent and presents themes drawn from the Sunday gospel readings, plus enriching devotions for family use. Appropriate for seasonal groups, small Christian communities, and individual reflection and prayer.

Year B: Take the Time: Encourages participants to prepare for Jesus' coming by setting aside everyday busyness and become more deeply aware of God's beckoning.

Year A: Trust the Lord: Urges participants to have confidence that God's challenging call is the true way to prepare for union with Christ.

Year C: Say Yes to God: Prompts participants to accept the invitation of Jesus' coming by reflecting on how to be more open to his presence in their lives.

Also available as an eBook!

For more information visit www.renewintl.org/seasonal

RENEW Small-Group Leader Series

Essentials for Small-Group Leaders

This book offers a comprehensive collection of pastoral insights and practical suggestions to help small community leaders guide their groups in a way that nourishes spiritual growth. Culled from RENEW International's almost four decades of experience in pioneering and promoting small Christian communities, this book overflows with simple but effective ideas and strategies that will enhance the way these groups reflect on and respond to the Gospel.

Leading Prayer in Small Groups

Have you ever been asked to lead prayer for your church group, council, or committee? RENEW International has developed a helpful resource called Leading Prayer in Small Groups to encourage you in leading fruitful group prayer experiences with confidence. *Leading Prayer in Small Groups* emphasizes the importance of group prayer for church groups of every kind and provides insight into why we pray. It also explains the role, qualities, and duties of a leader of prayer. Readers are guided through the stages of preparing group prayer and the process of effectively leading prayer for a group.

Visit www.renewintl.org/leaders to learn more or to order.

RENEW Scripture Series

Luke: My Spirit Rejoices!

Luke: My Spirit Rejoices! is the first book in the RENEW Scripture Series. Written by scripture scholar Martin Lang, this faith-sharing book engages readers with the entire Gospel and includes reflections on the content of the Gospel, the human behavior illuminated in Luke's work, and the Old Testament background for each passage. Sharing questions and opportunities to apply the gospel message to daily life make this a perfect resource for small Christian communities. Can be used individually or in a group.

Matthew: Come Follow Me

The Gospel of Matthew is the first book in the New Testament, a distinction

that reflects high value the Church has placed on this Gospel for nearly two thousand years. *Matthew: Come Follow Me* explores this unique account of the ministry, passion, and glorification of Jesus. Written by Scripture scholar Martin Lang, each chapter includes reflections on the Gospel plus sharing questions and examples of how the teaching of Jesus may apply to our everyday lives. This is a perfect resource for small groups, for personal reflection, or for homily preparation.

For more information go to www.renewintl.org/scripture

Spirituality for Everyday Life
with Ronald Rolheiser

Based on best-selling author Ronald Rolheiser, OMI's books *The Shattered Lantern, The Holy Longing,* and *Sacred Fire,* the *Spirituality for Everyday Life* with Ronald Rolheiser Series explores the phases of discipleship and how to live as Christ's disciples in today's world.

Longing for the Holy

Longing for the Holy is for those who want to enrich their sense of the presence of God. Designed for either a small group faith-sharing experience or personal reflection, participants explore the implications of the central mysteries of faith—the Incarnation, the Eucharist, and the Paschal Mystery —for spirituality. Attending to the cultural challenges that keep us from realizing our true desire, it considers the important themes of church community, justice, sexuality, the practices of the spiritual life, and being a mystic of the everyday.

Living in the Sacred

Living in the Sacred is a follow-up faith-sharing resource for *Longing for the Holy* and is based on Ronald Rolheiser's, *Sacred Fire. Living in the Sacred* takes participants on a deeper spiritual journey exploring the second stage of discipleship: "Giving your life away". Having moved through the "getting your life together" stage participants have made life commitments either in marriage or other relationships, child raising, to sick or elderly parents or other relatives, careers, communities, etc. *Living in the Sacred* is about how we stay true to these commitments as disciples of Christ.

For more information visit www.renewintl.org/spirituality

Creation at the Crossroads:
A Small-Group Resource on Pope Francis' "On Care for Our Common Home (Laudato Si')"

Creation at the Crossroads offers twelve faith-sharing sessions that respond to Pope Francis' call to action in his encyclical on ecology, Laudato Si'. Participants will internalize, and set as a priority in their lives, the Church's teaching on the care of creation and the impact of environmental change on the poor and vulnerable with this small-group resource.

Through Scripture, prayer, reflections, faith-sharing questions, and practical ideas for protecting and caring for the environment and people, this resource will move Catholics to faith-based action. Ideal for use in parishes, small groups, and campus ministries.

For more information go to www.renewintl.org/renewearth

At Prayer with Mary

At Prayer with Mary offers seven sessions on the life and mystery of Mary that will deepen your appreciation of and devotion to our Blessed Mother Mary and enrich your prayer experiences. Over the centuries, Mary's example has inspired Christians to imitate her by saying "yes" to God's call in their own lives. Her faithfulness, as it is portrayed in the Gospel narratives, is a model of the prayerful kind of life Jesus calls us to. Scripture, Catholic teaching, personal testimonies, and Marian prayer—including the rosary—provide a renewed appreciation of Mary's place in today's world, where she, as always, points the way to Christ.

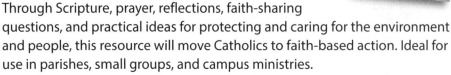

ALSO AN

BOOK

Also available as an eBook!

This 14-song CD is also available and contains the songs suggested for use during the moments of prayer.

Disponible en español: *No temas, María*

Connect with us!

Now it's easier than ever to connect with the RENEW International community for daily spiritual insights and updates.

 www.facebook.com/RENEWIntl

 blog.renewintl.org

 @RENEWIntl

 YouTube.com/user/RENEWInternational

Transform your Lenten alms into life-saving aid around the world. Give to CRS Rice Bowl:

crsricebowl.org/transform